FAITHFUL DOUBT

HABAKKUK

TRAVIS SCOTT

Is it faith or doubt? Or could it be "faithful doubt"? Yes. Like Travis Scott, I believe it is spiritually healthy and intellectually honest to practice faithful doubt in our broken and incorrigible world. Genuine Christians are faithful but also question the faithfulness of God, especially in the face of suffering. The obscure prophet Habakkuk is such a believer in Yahweh who practiced faithful doubt. By examining this prophet's eyewitness testimony of his people's suffering, Pastor Scott carefully, theologically, biblically, and pastorally points us to the One whom we can stubbornly believe in and honestly doubt.

Luke Bobo
Director of Strategic Partnerships, Made to Flourish

At some point in life, all of us are found asking, "Where is God in the midst of my sorrow?" The short book of Habakkuk addresses this question with powerful force. In the prophet's honest expressions of sorrow, confusion, and at times frustration, we find that having questions or doubt isn't the same as unbelief. In his book, Travis Scott helps walk us through this tension with great pastoral care. Through the inclusion of personal application questions at the end of each chapter, Scott gives us space to explore our own fear, faith, doubt and disappointment— all while pointing us back to the trustworthy faithfulness of the Lord. His work is easily accessible and a great resource for us all.

Becky Kiern
Author, *Our Light and Life: Identity in the Claims of Christ*

Many who have endured seasons of serious doubt about God, especially concerning his claim to be both sovereign and good at all times, have emerged not with a wrecked faith but a deeper, stronger one. The often-overlooked ancient prophet, Habakkuk, in both his words and his example, provides a model picture of such a person. As a student of Scripture and fellow struggler, Travis does an excellent job of introducing us to the prophet and his faithful, doubting journey. I am deeply encouraged by this work and trust that you will be also.

Scott Sauls
Pastor, Christ Presbyterian Church
Author, *Jesus Outside the Lines: A Gentle Answer*

This book is for everyone who has ever questioned the apparent inaction of God. It will help us to see our doubts as an invitation to a deeper relationship with God, one that draws us toward his character, his words, and his grace.

Jeff Kerr
Pastor, Crestwood Presbyterian Church

John Coltrane is my favorite jazz musician. His particular genius, in my opinion, is his masterful use of dissonance. His piercing and shocking notes bring us into the story of the song. It brings us into the story of life. Even the Christian life. Pastor Travis Scott writes, "Christians live with the cognitive dissonance of believing in God and yet having a lot of questions and doubts about him." I am thankful for this book. I am thankful to God for showing us through Habakkuk that doubt is not antithetical to faith. I'm thankful to Pastor Scott for inviting us into the rhythm of faithful doubt.

Irwyn Ince
Author, *The Beautiful Community*

God invites us to faith, but can such faith bear the weight of my serious doubts? Can God? In a manner reminiscent of the Psalms, the prophet Habakkuk exhibits the striking range of honest responses God's people can, and should, have to the painful realities of life in a broken world. The Lord is not troubled by our honesty; our doubts illumine the width and depth of God's grace. Travis Scott has produced a little book brimming with pastoral wisdom and Christ-centered hope for all of us who, with Habakkuk, are well-acquainted with everything that is wrong and impatient for God's justice and peace.

Kenneth J. Woo
Associate Professor of Church History, Pittsburgh Theo-logical Seminary

Long live the Minor Prophets! Too many pastors and churches ignore these prophetic books, but they are important for us to read to understand the whole counsel of God. Travis Scott helps one of the most fascinating books in all of Scripture come alive with this thoughtful commentary. He shows how Habakkuk complains *to* God instead of *about* God, and why that's so important. Scott writes for pastors and Bible teachers needing good resources, but he also writes for anyone wanting to understand the Old Testament better. This volume is another in a line of solid Christ-centered biblical studies, very readable and applicable to modern life.

Jonathan Dorst
Pastor, RiverOaks Tulsa

With his characteristic clarity, Travis Scott explores Habakkuk's raw message of doubtful exasperation turned to reverent trust for anyone who wonders if God listens, cares, and acts. Travis offers helpful takeaways and reflection questions as he carefully guides the reader through the text. Travis' heartening reminder to practice a "remembering faith" encourages the reader to trust the God who ultimately answered Habakkuk's "How long, O LORD?" through the life, death, resurrection, and anticipated return of Jesus Christ.

Donald C. Guthrie
Professor, Trinity Evangelical Divinity School

Like Habakkuk, we are living through extreme circumstances and the wiser among us know that more is on the way. Like all of God's servants, the enemy of our soul delights to take up such circumstances and tempt us toward discouragement and doubt. While the combination of these pressures—extreme circumstances and our enemy's temptation to doubt—will either move us toward God or move us away from him, readers of this volume will find no rigid formula for beating back honest questions nor any word of rebuke for struggling with genuine hesitancy and fear. Readers will find, however, committed biblical exposition, hard won pastoral wisdom, and every encouragement towards "faithful doubt" as a pathway to a more robust faith that simultaneously wrestles and rests.

Mark P. Ryan
Director, Francis A. Schaeffer Institute, Covenant Theological Seminary

Whereas most Christians are probably unfamiliar with the biblical book Habakkuk, I'm confident most of us are familiar with doubt. This doubt is often unspoken, unwanted, and untreated, which can lead to disillusionment and, tragically, even disbelief. It doesn't have to be this way, as Travis Scott reminds us. By looking through the lens of God's faithful, yet doubtful, servant Habakkuk, Travis guides us through grappling with the reality of "faithful doubt" in ways that can (and should) ultimately lead us closer to God. This book showcases Travis' tremendous capacity for empathy, relatability, pastoral care, and boldness in addressing real issues that often go unaddressed. It's a wonderful gift to the many of us who struggle to process our own doubts faithfully.

Scott Manor
President, Professor, Knox Theological Seminary

Habakkuk could not believe what he was seeing, nor could he understand it. He had lots of questions for his Lord. Have you ever felt that way? The Holy Spirit has preserved Habakkuk's complaints as a model for us to have such painful conversations with God ourselves. If you lead

Bible studies or pastor a congregation like Travis Scott, his guided tour through Habakkuk's prayer journal will help you create space to hear the pain, doubt, and questions that honest people have in a time of sickness, grief and relational breakdown. *Faithful Doubt* models the primary practices of ministry in good order by legitimizing questions, listening well to the hurting, then praying to the One who can answer and heal.

Gregory R. Perry
Vice President of Strategic Projects, Third Millennium Ministries

These are trying times for believers and unbelievers alike. We live in a world where injustice, destruction and violence stalk not just the streets of foreign cities but of our own. Some days the news is so trying we wonder if we can bear the weight of the brokenness. We wonder where God is, if he notices or cares and whether he is doing anything to right wrong, reverse injustice and promote equality. Christians can be troubled when such doubts arise, fearing for the health of their faith. Travis Scott, a pastor who believes Christ speaks as Lord into every situation shows that many centuries ago a Hebrew prophet, Habakkuk, wrestled with the same questions. He had the audacity to question God—accuse him, really—and in a wonder of grace, God did not rebuke him but took the time to answer. *Faithful Doubt* is a book for twenty-first century believers that asks us to listen in on a raw, refreshing and life-giving conversation between a troubled prophet and a listening, surprising, active God. It helps us see doubt and faith realistically and biblically, provides a model of hearing Scripture as God's word, and is a bracing alternative to the doom-scrolling that breeds doubt, pessimism and little else.

Denis Haack
Director, Ransom Fellowship

CONTENTS

*To all those who have deeply blessed me by
sharing your doubts and struggles.
Your openness and vulnerability have made
me a better pastor and a better human.
This work, for what it's worth, is dedicated to you all.*

*Special thanks to Chris and Jesse at the Bulldog,
my favorite spot for drinking, thinking, and writing.
Your friendship and banter keep me grounded.*

PREFACE

For I do not seek to understand in order
that I may believe,
but I believe in order to understand.
For this also I believe—
that unless I believe I shall not understand.
—St. Anselm

After I finished seminary, my wife, Brooke, and I spent three months in New Zealand exploring ministry opportunities. Our time there would eventually lead to a calling to plant a church in central Auckland. However, those three months were a trying time for me as I had entered seminary silently telling God I wasn't going to be a pastor, I wasn't going to raise money, and I definitely wasn't going to go overseas.

Yet there I was overseas contemplating raising support to live and pastor there long-term. More trying was the fact that the initial opportunity we'd gone to New Zealand to explore was very obviously not a good fit, and for a time we were left wondering what in the world we were doing on the other side of the planet. God had completely turned my plans for life on their head, and I wasn't really sure of much about myself or my calling anymore. Had I made a huge mistake? Whatever God was up to, I didn't understand it at the time. There was also a nagging question constantly lurking beneath the surface: Was God even in this at all?

As trying as those three months were for me, they were far worse for Brooke. She had all the same culture shock and questions about our future as I did, but she had something much worse—too much time on her hands to think about it all. Having the time itself was very frustrating for her. My wife is incredibly gifted. She is a capable administrator, organizer, communicator, teacher, and disciple-maker. But when we originally got to New Zealand, her gifts and skills were not being used or fully appreciated. There really wasn't much for her to do, and this led to something of an existential crisis for her as she had to wrestle through her own calling and purpose. In the midst of that internal struggle, she began to wrestle with bigger questions of faith and belief.

I knew she was struggling, but I wasn't aware of the depth and extent of that struggle. Towards the end of our three months we took a road trip through the length of New Zealand seeing the sites and visiting local churches to get a better picture of the denomination in which we were working. We hoped this trip would show us if there might be a place for us in that beautiful country.

One afternoon during our road trip, we were driving through some of the most amazing scenery imaginable.

We'd spent time admiring the Southern Alps from across Lake Tekapo and were driving further into those Alps to see the highest point within New Zealand, Aoraki/Mt. Cook. Surrounded by breathtaking beauty my breath was taken away inside our little car for a very different reason. In the midst of an argument we were having, Brooke stated she wasn't sure what she believed about God anymore or if she believed in him at all.

I was stunned.

How did I respond? Like a typical student straight out of seminary—poorly. Worse than poorly. As I think back on this conversation, I'd say I completely failed her. She had opened up with a deep, vulnerable honesty about her personal struggle and doubt, and I freaked out.

I don't remember my exact words, but I know I didn't listen to her well. I tried to fix her problem instead wrestling through it with her. I treated her questions and doubt as a problem to be solved, something to be patched up with dry intellectual answers and put behind us. Because of that, I gave her answers devoid of true empathy. In all honesty this wasn't just a moment of failing to love and care for Brooke in her moment of pain and struggle (thought it definitely was that!). It was also a moment which revealed my own gaping hypocrisy.

I had come to greatly admire the work of Francis Schaeffer who founded the organization known as L'Abri[1] with his wife Edith. One of Schaeffer's great mottos was "Honest answers to honest questions," and I loved it, or at least the idea of it. I had focused my studies on evangelism, apologetics, and cultural engagement. I was all about dealing with doubts, at least theoretically.

But doubt looks different when it's sitting next to you in the car. It looks different when it comes from the mouth of the person you love more than any other. In a moment like that, doubt was more difficult and scary because it was not a theoretical problem. It was unavoidably real. This wasn't a philosophical apologetic problem. These were personal questions borne out of pain and frustration. And because my wife is who she is, it was doubt that was honest enough to cut through my insufficient answers.

I'd like to tell you I figured it out and eventually discovered the best things to say to help her. I didn't.

Her true Comforter helped her in ways I couldn't. Over time he spoke peace to her heart and gave her a renewed confidence in the Gospel and what it meant for her identity as a daughter of God. I didn't fix Brookes's doubts, but God used her doubts to fix something in me. Her genuine, vulnerable struggling through her questions and sense of God's absence opened me up to be more honest about my own doubts.

Ultimately God used this time to humble me and better prepare me for a ministry marked by helping people wrestle through their own questions and doubts about God and the Christian Gospel. Instead of trying to beat away doubts with rationalistic formulas and canned answers, I've learned to encourage people to lay hold of God through faith in the midst of those doubts and questions.

As a minister, I've come to see the practice of faithful doubt as necessary for a healthy spiritual life. That might sound like a nonsense statement to some. Many Christians think the presence of doubt cancels out faith or makes them somehow unworthy to receive grace. The problem with this way of thinking is that it does nothing to eliminate doubt and questions. It just buries them so they can be hidden.

When we aren't honest about our doubts and questions they are never actually addressed and end up doing more to damage to us. We give doubt more power when we treat it as something that can never be admitted. Similarly, many non-Christians I've talked with have bought into this way of thinking. I've had friends say things to me like, "I could never believe. I have too many doubts." They think faith is the absence of doubt, so they assume they couldn't have faith because they have so much doubt. Yet, faith and doubt are not the polar opposites we often think they are.

If we read through Scripture, we find the puzzling fact that doubts and questions about God and his ways are actually quite prevalent. In that sense the entire book of Habakkuk could be described as one man's wrestling with God and boldly stating his questions and doubts. Habakkuk and other biblical authors show us an important truth: Sometimes the strongest faith is the one most honest about its doubts. Habakkuk, and those other biblical authors, teach us that the healthiest thing for a believer to do is to be faithful with their doubt. We are called to entrust (the true meaning of faith) our doubts to the One we simultaneously believe in yet struggle to believe in.

This short book originally began as an even shorter sermon series.[2] However, its real origin is based in the rough and tumble of doing life and ministry in the real world. It comes from the privilege of having had men and women be courageous enough to be honest with me about their own struggles in this area. God has worked through all these people to open my own eyes to read his Word more faithfully and to see that he works in us through our doubt. I write this for the many people I've talked with who struggle with doubts of various kinds. And the many like them who think they could never tell their pastor about those doubts and struggles. I write this because my own faith is often a great battle of trust in the midst of doubts.

This book is written primarily with Christians in mind, particularly Christians who may be struggling with what to do with their questions and doubts. However, I also hope that anyone curious about the Christian faith may be encouraged from this work by learning more about how Christian believers handle their doubts. I pray the honesty about doubts discussed here might make the idea of faith in Christ seem like a more plausible proposition for some.

Many Christians live with the cognitive dissonance of believing in God and yet having a lot of questions and doubts about him. The dissonance comes because they've often been told to "just believe," and their doubts and questions have been stuffed down inside instead of dealt with honestly. Many non-Christians have avoided the faith because they think that to become a Christian means to have 100 percent certainty, and they wrestle way too much with the God of the Bible to be able to claim that. By studying the book of Habakkuk, we learn that the proper expression of doubt can not only be healthy—it can be a major act of faith. Questions and struggles aren't something to be ignored or avoided but embraced head on and taken to God himself.

What follows is not an in depth biblical commentary or a detailed exegetical exploration of the book of Habakkuk. It's also not a carefully articulated philosophical or theological exploration of suffering or the problem of evil (though it touches on those important topics). There are people far more skilled than me who've already written those works.

Instead, I hope this book gives you pastoral permission to take a deep breath and realize you're not alone in your questions. I hope it helps you realize it's okay to struggle with doubts. More than okay—it's actually a spiritually fruitful thing! I hope in these pages you find some help for how to approach our own questions and uncertainties about the faith. Ultimately though, I hope you are pointed to the One in whom we can find comfort in the midst of doubt.

———————————————

1. "L'Abri" is French for "shelter" and the Schaeffers' desired to make their home a place of shelter for people struggling with the big questions of life, faith, and God. For more information on the history and continued ministry of L'Abri visit labri.org.
2. "Wrestling with God: Lessons from Habakkuk," Grace & Peace, PCA, last modified March 25, 2018, http://graceandpeacepgh.org/sermons/series/wrestling-with-god:-lessons-from-habakkuk.

INTRODUCTION TO HABAKKUK

I'm guessing the book of Habakkuk probably isn't one you're incredibly familiar with. It's not on many people's list of Top Ten Books of the Bible. It's a short book that gets passed over, and it's a part of a group of other short books that tend to get passed over even by serious readers of the Bible.

Habakkuk is one of the twelve books known as the Minor Prophets. The adjective "minor" here simply means they are not long books like the Major Prophets (Isaiah, Jeremiah, Ezekiel, and Daniel). Yet the Minor Prophets do tend to be unintentionally neglected by a lot of Christians and therefore become de facto "minor" in importance.

This sentiment was humorously highlighted in an article posted on a satirical Christian website entitled "The TL;DR Edition Of All 66 Books Of The Bible."[1] For those who don't know "TL;DR" stands for "Too long; didn't read." The article boasts, "Forget about reading through the Bible in a year—now you can read through the Bible in about five minutes!" It then proceeds to give a sarcastic one-sentence summary of each book of the Bible.

When you get to the minor prophets, all of them, except for Jonah but including Habakkuk, have this description: "Minor prophet who's not Jonah—feel free to skip." This is one of those moments where we might declare that it's funny because it's true. We tend to feel free to skip over the Minor Prophets instead of doing the hard work of understanding them.

However, the Minor Prophets should not be skipped. When we dive into them, we find they are relevant, powerful books. The Minor Prophets deal with issues of justice—how faith should guide a person's care for their society and the most vulnerable members of that society. They attack superficial and hypocritical religion. They warn against marrying faith to politics and societal expectations. They wrestle with perennial questions like the problem of evil. They talk about how God is working in the midst of suffering and the question of if God even is working in the midst of suffering. They face all these things head on and hold forth the promise of redemption in some of the darkest circumstances. When properly understood, the Minor Prophets are powerful books that expose our hearts and call us to deeper faith. Habakkuk is no exception.

Even those familiar with the Bible might find Habakkuk difficult to digest because the language and tone can seem quite foreign to what we're used to with more popular or well-known sections of the Scripture. And yet Habakkuk is a part of God's inspired communication to humanity. It has helpful and encouraging things to say to us.

However, before we jump into the text itself, we should know something about the historical and cultural context into which the book was originally written.

Habakkuk was written sometime between 640 and 598 BC, which means the prophet Habakkuk was a contemporary of the prophets Zephaniah and Jeremiah. The period of time when these prophets were ministering and writing was one in which God's people weren't doing so hot. To put it simply, lots of messed up things were going on with God's people and had been for a while.

About 300 years before the writing of Habakkuk, the nation of Israel had split into two different kingdoms.[2] Israel (it retained the name of the previous whole, united kingdom) was the northern kingdom, and the kingdom of Judah was in the south. These two nations had recurring strife and war with one another, yet, while these kingdoms of separated brothers were at odds and diverged in significant ways, there was a gradual slide toward the same types of unfaithfulness and rebellion against God in both.

Throughout this time, the practice of false religion and idolatry was prevalent. These problems caused social tension and the unravelling of cultural and spiritual norms designed by God to ensure equity and security for all segments of society. In Northern Israel you see a pretty steady progression of kings who get worse and worse and worse, and as the king went, so went the nation. The whole of Israel gets more wicked, more corrupt, more idolatrous, more faithless, and more rebellious against God.

All this was despite God's constant warnings to them. Most of the biblical writings during this time period consist of God's constant pleading with his people to turn from their destructive ways and turn back to him, but they don't. Instead, they plug their ears to his voice and finally about one hundred years before Habakkuk is written, the Northern Kingdom is completely destroyed. God sends the Assyrian empire to punish them for their betrayal and rebellion, and they are wiped out and taken into exile (2 Kings 17).

The southern kingdom of Judah, where Habakkuk conducted his ministry, had a slightly different pattern with its kings. Judah went back and forth between godly kings who ruled well and ungodly kings who ruled... not so well.

Judah was the same as Israel in the sense that as the king went, so went the people. When they had godly kings leading them, the nation flourished and did well. But when they had faithless kings guiding them, they spiraled into cultural, ethical, and spiritual dissipation. While there were bright moments in the life of Judah, they too experienced a steady decline and slide into corruption and decay. This also came despite God's constant warnings through other prophets and what they saw happen to the Northern Kingdom.

When Habakkuk writes his prophecy, the king reigning in Jerusalem was named Jehoiakim. Jehoiakim was a bad king, one of the worst.

In fact, Jehoiakim wasn't even really a king. He was a

puppet. A little earlier in their history, Judah had gone to war against Egypt and lost. Big time.

Their king was killed and Pharaoh Neco of Egypt placed Jehoahaz (Joehoiakim's father) on the throne in Jerusalem as his vassal king, a king who was more amenable to Egyptian interests. Pharaoh Neco eventually got sick of Jehoahaz and imprisoned him. He then placed his son Jehoiakim on the throne. (2 Kings 23:28–37).

Under Jehoiakim, there was increased corruption and idolatry throughout Judea because as the king went, so went the people. During this period more people in Judah walked away from God and turned their back on his ways.

When Habakkuk writes his prophecy, it's during what is probably one of the lowest points in Judah's history. They are past the point of no return, and their judgment (which is prophesied in Habakkuk 1) comes just ten to fifteen years later when the Babylonians lay siege to Jerusalem and destroy the temple in 587 BC (2 Kings 25).

It's important to understand at least some of this if you want to understand the tone and message of Habakkuk. These three short chapters are filled with the strain and frustration of a prophet watching his people fall apart. He is the messenger of God called to speak to people who don't want to listen.

We'll see that in the midst of this most difficult of callings, Habakkuk also comes to question if God is even listening to him anymore. Try to keep these things in mind as you read the prophecy of Habakkuk. Even if the history and cultural context of Habakkuk is lost on many of us, the main questions he's struggling with are questions all of us can relate to: Is God even listening? Does he really care?

---

1. "The TL;DR Edition Of All 66 Books Of The Bible," The Babylon Bee, last modified February 15, 2018, https://babylonbee.com/news/the-tldr-edition-of-all-66-books-of-the-bible.
2. You can read the history of this division in the biblical books of 1 and 2 Kings as well as 2 Chronicles.

THE PROPHECY OF HABAKKUK

As I mentioned in the introduction, Habakkuk is most likely not a book you're overly familiar with. It's quite possible you've never read it and even more likely that you've never heard it read out loud.

For that reason I'd encourage you to read it right now. I've seen similar encouragements to read particular portions of Scripture in many books. The author urges you to put his book down and go read Scripture first.

Honestly, I hardly ever set the book down and go read the portion of the Bible they encourage me to.

Therefore—and since the book of Habakkuk is short—I'm including it here. You don't even have to put this book down.

Take a few minutes to read Habakkuk in its entirety. If you want to get an even better sense of the tone of the book, try reading it out loud. Unless of course you're sitting in a pub, café, or some other public place—because that would be weird.

In order to understand the general flow of Habakkuk,

it might be helpful to understand the basic outline before you read.

The main thing to note about Habakkuk is that chapters 1 and 2 are a dialogue between the prophet and God.

In 1:2–4, Habakkuk offers a first complaint to God.

1:5–11 is God's first reply.

Habakkuk then responds to God with a second complaint in 1:12–2:1.

He receives a second reply from God in 2:2–20.

In Chapter 3, Habakkuk concludes his prophecy with a song of faith.

Those are the basics. Now you can read the prophecy. This is the word of the Lord:[1]

———

1:1 The oracle that Habakkuk the prophet saw.

2 O LORD,[2] how long shall I cry for help,
  and you will not hear?
Or cry to you "Violence!"
  and you will not save?
3 Why do you make me see iniquity,
  and why do you idly look at wrong?
Destruction and violence are before me;
  strife and contention arise.
4 So the law is paralyzed,
  and justice never goes forth.
For the wicked surround the righteous;
  so justice goes forth perverted.

5 "Look among the nations, and see;

wonder and be astounded.
For I am doing a work in your days
  that you would not believe if told.
⁶ *For behold, I am raising up the Chaldeans,*
  that bitter and hasty nation,
who march through the breadth of the earth,
  to seize dwellings not their own.
⁷ *They are dreaded and fearsome;*
  their justice and dignity go forth from themselves.
⁸ *Their horses are swifter than leopards,*
  more fierce than the evening wolves;
  their horsemen press proudly on.
Their horsemen come from afar;
  they fly like an eagle swift to devour.
⁹ *They all come for violence,*
  all their faces forward.
  They gather captives like sand.
¹⁰ *At kings they scoff,*
  and at rulers they laugh.
They laugh at every fortress,
  for they pile up earth and take it.
¹¹ *Then they sweep by like the wind and go on,*
  guilty men, whose own might is their god!

¹² *Are you not from everlasting,*
  O LORD my God, my Holy One?
   We shall not die.
O LORD, you have ordained them as a judgment,
  and you, O Rock, have established them for reproof.
¹³ *You who are of purer eyes than to see evil*
  and cannot look at wrong,

why do you idly look at traitors
    and remain silent when the wicked swallows up
    the man more righteous than he?
14 You make mankind like the fish of the sea,
    like crawling things that have no ruler.
15 He brings all of them up with a hook;
    he drags them out with his net;
he gathers them in his dragnet;
    so he rejoices and is glad.
16 Therefore he sacrifices to his net
    and makes offerings to his dragnet;
for by them he lives in luxury,
    and his food is rich.
17 Is he then to keep on emptying his net
    and mercilessly killing nations forever?
2:1 I will take my stand at my watchpost
    and station myself on the tower,
and look out to see what he will say to me,
    and what I will answer concerning my complaint.

2 And the LORD answered me:
"Write the vision;
make it plain on tablets,
    so he may run who reads it.
3 For still the vision awaits its appointed time;
    it hastens to the end—it will not lie.
If it seems slow, wait for it;
    it will surely come; it will not delay.
4 "Behold, his soul is puffed up; it is not upright
within him,
    but the righteous shall live by his faith.

⁵ "Moreover, wine is a traitor,
  an arrogant man who is never at rest.
His greed is as wide as Sheol;
  like death he has never enough.
He gathers for himself all nations
  and collects as his own all peoples."
⁶ Shall not all these take up their taunt against him, with
scoffing and riddles for him,
and say,
"Woe to him who heaps up what is not his own—
    for how long?—
    and loads himself with pledges!"
⁷ Will not your debtors suddenly arise,
    and those awake who will make you tremble?
    Then you will be spoil for them.
⁸ Because you have plundered many nations,
    all the remnant of the peoples shall plunder you,
for the blood of man and violence to the earth,
    to cities and all who dwell in them.
⁹ "Woe to him who gets evil gain for his house,
  to set his nest on high,
    to be safe from the reach of harm!
¹⁰ You have devised shame for your house
  by cutting off many peoples;
    you have forfeited your life.
¹¹ For the stone will cry out from the wall,
    and the beam from the woodwork respond.
¹² "Woe to him who builds a town with blood
    and founds a city on iniquity!
¹³ Behold, is it not from the Lord of hosts
    that peoples labor merely for fire,

and nations weary themselves for nothing?
¹⁴ For the earth will be filled
    with the knowledge of the glory of the LORD
    as the waters cover the sea.
¹⁵ "Woe to him who makes his neighbors drink—
    you pour out your wrath and make them drunk,
    in order to gaze at their nakedness!
¹⁶ You will have your fill of shame instead of glory.
    Drink, yourself, and show your uncircumcision!
The cup in the Lord's right hand
    will come around to you,
    and utter shame will come upon your glory!
¹⁷ The violence done to Lebanon will overwhelm you,
    as will the destruction of the beasts that terrified them,
for the blood of man and violence to the earth,
    to cities and all who dwell in them.
¹⁸ "What profit is an idol
    when its maker has shaped it,
    a metal image, a teacher of lies?
For its maker trusts in his own creation
    when he makes speechless idols!
¹⁹ Woe to him who says to a wooden thing, Awake;
    to a silent stone, Arise!
Can this teach?
Behold, it is overlaid with gold and silver,
    and there is no breath at all in it.
²⁰ But the LORD is in his holy temple;
    let all the earth keep silence before him."

^{3:1}A prayer of Habakkuk the prophet, according to
Shigionoth.³

2 O LORD, I have heard the report of you,
  and your work, O LORD, do I fear.
In the midst of the years revive it;
  in the midst of the years make it known;
  in wrath remember mercy.
3 God came from Teman,
  and the Holy One from Mount Paran. [Selah]4
His splendor covered the heavens,
  and the earth was full of his praise.
4 His brightness was like the light;
  rays flashed from his hand;
  and there he veiled his power.
5 Before him went pestilence,
  and plague followed at his heels.
6 He stood and measured the earth;
  he looked and shook the nations;
then the eternal mountains were scattered;
  the everlasting hills sank low.
  His were the everlasting ways.
7 I saw the tents of Cushan in affliction;
  the curtains of the land of Midian did tremble.
8 Was your wrath against the rivers, O LORD?
  Was your anger against the rivers,
  or your indignation against the sea,
when you rode on your horses,
  on your chariot of salvation?
9 You stripped the sheath from your bow,
  calling for many arrows. [Selah]
You split the earth with rivers.
10 The mountains saw you and writhed;
  the raging waters swept on;

the deep gave forth its voice;
   it lifted its hands on high.
11 The sun and moon stood still in their place
   at the light of your arrows as they sped,
   at the flash of your glittering spear.
12 You marched through the earth in fury;
   you threshed the nations in anger.
13 You went out for the salvation of your people,
   for the salvation of your anointed.
You crushed the head of the house of the wicked,
   laying him bare from thigh to neck. [Selah]
14 You pierced with his own arrows the heads of his
warriors,
   who came like a whirlwind to scatter me,
   rejoicing as if to devour the poor in secret.
15 You trampled the sea with your horses,
   the surging of mighty waters.
16 I hear, and my body trembles;
   my lips quiver at the sound;
rottenness enters into my bones;
   my legs tremble beneath me.
Yet I will quietly wait for the day of trouble
   to come upon people who invade us.
17 Though the fig tree should not blossom,
   nor fruit be on the vines,
the produce of the olive fail
   and the fields yield no food,
the flock be cut off from the fold
   and there be no herd in the stalls,
18 yet I will rejoice in the LORD;
   I will take joy in the God of my salvation.

¹⁹ GOD, the Lord, is my strength;
  he makes my feet like the deer's;
  he makes me tread on my high places.

To the choirmaster: with stringed instruments.
—Habakkuk 1:1-3:19

---

1. Scripture quotations are from the ESV® Bible (The Holy Bible, English Standard Version®), copyright © 2001 by Crossway, a publishing ministry of Good News Publishers. Used by permission. All rights reserved.
2. When you see the words "Lord" or "God" in all caps in the Old Testament it is the Translator following the tradition of translating the personal name of God "Yahweh" in a more formal manner.
3. The exact meaning of *Shigionoth* is unknown. It is only used in two places in the Bible. It could refer to a type of instrumentation or style of music.
4. Similar to *Shigionoth*, the meaning of the word *Selah* is uncertain. It is used most often in the Psalms and is thought to be some sort of musical or liturgical direction. It is therefore often unspoken when reading Scripture.

THE PROPHET'S BURDEN
HABAKKUK 1:1–2:1

Life is pain, highness. Anyone who tells you different is selling something.
—Wesley, *The Princess Bride*

Some Christians have formed the idea that Christianity and the Christian life are furnished with flowers and tranquillity. When faced with difficulties and tragedies they start wondering about the strength and validity of their faith, and it benefits them in such circumstances to express to God in all honesty and transparency how they feel, whether it's a question, complaint, disappointment, doubt or feelings of despair. It would benefit them to learn from Habakkuk that God wants them to share all they think or feel, whether they consider that stemming from faith, little faith or even complete lack of faith.
—Riad A. Kassis, *Frustrated with God: A Syrian Theologian's Reflections on Habakkuk*

It seems like every generation thinks less of the generation which comes after it. The older generation claims the newer one is ruining the country, and those claims tend to begin again as soon as the younger generation becomes the older. It's easy to dismiss the values and desires of folks when they differ or conflict with your own.

Often complaints about societal breakdown are really a hearkening back to some imagined golden age that never really existed. And yet, there is such a thing as societal breakdown. History has seen the rise and fall of many nations, and the strongest seem to fall only after they've defeated themselves through moral decay and internal chaos.

In the introduction, we saw that Habakkuk is writing to a nation at its lowest spiritual and social point. He writes about this situation in the opening section of his prophecy. It would be easy to read these opening verses in Habakkuk as a description of wickedness in general and the problems of bad people out there in the world somewhere. However, keep in mind that in verses 1:2–4 Habakkuk is describing what *God's people* are like, and he says they are horrible.

Habakkuk says he's crying out to God because there is violence and destruction all around him (1:2–3). In addition to violence and destruction, he says the land is filled with strife and contention (1:3). One commentator draws out some of the meaning here. He writes:

> The [violence, or] "plundering" encompassed any forced act including but not limited to kidnapping in all its forms, slavery, human trafficking… The word

'contention' refers to complaints and lawsuits. The word 'strife' refers to conflicts, whether between individuals, communities or peoples.[1]

Habakkuk is condemning the people of God because, instead of being a nation of peace, they have become a place of strife. The strong prey on the weak, even to the point of enslavement and subjugation. In addition to actual physical violence, everyone is suing everyone. The court docket is full, but the problem is the courts are filled with injustice. They've become the place where the rich win. That's not justice. It's not right. It doesn't matter if you have the just plea or the just cause. You can't go to the courts because the "law is paralyzed" (1:4).

The law of God was supposed to guide the people of God into peace and justice, but the rulers and even the religious authorities have abandoned God and his word. So Habakkuk says the law is paralyzed. It's unable to help the cause of justice. This is a time when the leaders were embracing false prophets who told them and the people exactly what they wanted to hear. They're paying to hear prophecies of ease and comfort instead of hard words like those in Habakkuk. Justice is paralyzed and perverted because no one is listening to God or truly seeking his instruction or correction.

This is where things are at with the people of God. They are enslaving and oppressing one another. People are destroying one another physically and financially. The rich are oppressing the poor. The strong are devastating the weak and vulnerable. Everyone is at each other's throats, and there is no recourse for the victims. Injustice, immorality, oppression, and death fill the land. The righteous are surrounded by the wicked like lambs for slaughter. And this is supposed to be the nation which represents the way of God in the world!

What Habakkuk is describing is a culture at war with itself, tearing itself apart. This leads Habakkuk into his conversation with God—which makes up the bulk of this prophecy. Habakkuk is distressed and troubled by what he sees going on all around him, and he cries out to God. It's worth noting that the word "oracle" in verse 1 can be more literally translated as "burden." It's fair to say these three chapters are the "burden" of Habakkuk. The tone of his prophecy confirms the burdensome nature of his experience.

For the rest of this chapter, I want us to explore two aspects of this burden: the burden of God's silence and the burden of God's answer.

The Burden of God's Silence

Obviously the cultural situation I've just described bothered and burdened Habakkuk. Remember that Habakkuk is a prophet of God. He cares about God's law and God's people. His whole job is to call people to faithfully listen and respond to what God has to say. And yet, he sees the people who should at least theoretically be the most open and responsive to God's instructions abandoning all concern with the things of God, and it distresses him.

But consider what distresses him more. In verses 2–4, we see the prophet describing all the problems and wickedness in Judah, but what is his actual complaint?

What is he most burdened by? It's the fact that God doesn't seem to notice or care. Look again at verses 2–3:

> ² *O LORD, how long shall I cry for help,*
>   *and you will not hear?*
> *Or cry to you "Violence!"*
>   *and you will not save?*
> ³ *Why do you make me see iniquity,*
>   *and why do you idly look at wrong?*
> *Destruction and violence are before me;*
>   *strife and contention arise.*

Do you hear what Habakkuk is saying? *"How long shall I cry?"* The question implies this has been a repeated prayer of the prophet. This isn't the first time he's asking, "What's up, God?" Habakkuk has been praying about this situation and crying for help over and over again, for a long time. He's asking:

How long?
How long must I continue to say these things to you?
How many times must I call to your attention how bad the situation has gotten?

This is not just prayer in some sort of formal, impersonal, and detached way. He's crying out! The Hebrew word for *cry* here might be better translated as *shout*. Habakkuk is so pained and troubled by all the pain and trouble he sees he's shouting at God about it. In 1:2–3 Habakkuk is saying,

Don't you see what I see?
I'm begging you to do something, begging you to help.
How long must I yell in pain before you will hear me?
Why don't you do something?
What is wrong with you?

His complaint is that God just doesn't seem to care. Habakkuk says God is forcing him to see all sorts of injustice and pain, and it's killing him. Meanwhile God seems indifferent. He is inactive and idle in the face of misery and pain. Habakkuk is a prophet called to deliver God's word, and yet no word from God comes to the prophet. Instead he is plagued and burdened by God's silence.

It would be easy to quickly read over these verses and miss their weight. This can be even easier to do because we tend to assume pious tones in the voices of those writing the Bible, especially when they're speaking to God. However, when you slow down and consider what Habakkuk is saying and how he's saying it, you see that these verses are heavy with the emotional weight and distress of prolonged crying out to God in the midst of pain and suffering with nothing in reply... except silence. Habakkuk is frustrated and angry with God at his silence. If I used the language and words that I know would adequately convey the emotional tone of this passage, most Christians would be shocked if not offended.

We have to hear this tone though.

We have to realize the emotional tone and weight of Habakkuk because so many of us feel the same way. We have experienced the same distress in the face of God's apparent silence—at least we do if we're paying attention.

All you have to do is follow the news headlines. Every day of every week seems to bring yet another horrible story of unthinkable pain and suffering. We live in a world where genocide doesn't cause us to blink anymore, where terrorists post videos of themselves beheading innocent victims—and average people watch!

Americans live in the midst of radical injustice, systemic racism, and oppression. The USA is called the land of the free, but many of my African American friends have legitimate concerns for their life when they are pulled over by the police, which seems to happen to many of them with a higher frequency than in my own experience.

There are a ton of other evils we're confronted with. We live in a culture where one in three women and one in four men will suffer sexual abuse or assault in their lifetime. We live in a culture where my young children have to go through active shooter training at their school. Then there is political corruption, clerical sex-abuse scandals, and a myriad of other issues, like the fact that in the time it's taken you to read this paragraph approximately 110 people will have died of starvation around the world.

And then there's the whole matter of global pandemics.

Beyond all this, there is the everyday suffering we see in the lives of our friends and loved ones. Maybe it's a battle with prolonged illness. Maybe it's the fractured relationships and lives marred by all sorts of betrayals and abandonments. And it's not just our friends. *We* suffer through these things and more. Life in this world comes with pain and tragedy. If we're honest, all of this makes us want to cry out with Habakkuk and shout at God:

Where are you?
Don't you care?
How long will you ignore our need?
Why don't you help?
Why don't you speak?
When evil is so loud why are you so silent?

This is the heavy burden of God's silence that weighs down on Habakkuk and causes him to shout out to God.

The Burden of God's Answer

Habakkuk is burdened by God's silence, and he cries and shouts out to him. Yet he becomes even more burdened by God's answer:

> *⁶ For behold, I am raising up the Chaldeans,*
> *that bitter and hasty nation,*
> *who march through the breadth of the earth,*
> *to seize dwellings not their own.*
> *⁷ They are dreaded and fearsome;*
> *their justice and dignity go forth from themselves.*
> *⁸ Their horses are swifter than leopards,*
> *more fierce than the evening wolves;*
> *their horsemen press proudly on.*
> *Their horsemen come from afar;*
> *they fly like an eagle swift to devour.*
> *⁹ They all come for violence,*

all their faces forward.
They gather captives like sand.
10 At kings they scoff,
and at rulers they laugh.
They laugh at every fortress,
for they pile up earth and take it.
11 Then they sweep by like the wind and go on,
guilty men, whose own might is their god!"
Habakkuk 1:6–11

We'll spend time later focusing in on some of the details of God's reply here and his next one in 2:2–20.

The summary of God's reply is that he too is troubled by all the wickedness and injustice he sees in Judah. He's saying, "Actually, I do see. I do hear. And I'm so upset by what I see happening, I'm bringing the Chaldeans to punish my wicked people. I'm going to bring judgment" (the Chaldeans are more popularly known as the Babylonians—therefore, I'll be referring to them as the Babylonians from here on out) .

This is not what Habakkuk expected to hear. The prophet complains again to God:

12 Are you not from everlasting,
O LORD my God, my Holy One?
We shall not die.
O LORD, you have ordained them as a judgment,
and you, O Rock, have established them for reproof.
13 You who are of purer eyes than to see evil
and cannot look at wrong,
why do you idly look at traitors

and remain silent when the wicked swallows up
the man more righteous than he?
14 You make mankind like the fish of the sea,
like crawling things that have no ruler.
15 He brings all of them up with a hook;
he drags them out with his net;
he gathers them in his dragnet;
so he rejoices and is glad.
16 Therefore he sacrifices to his net
and makes offerings to his dragnet;
for by them he lives in luxury,
and his food is rich.
17 Is he then to keep on emptying his net
and mercilessly killing nations forever?
Habakkuk 1:12–17

In essence, Habakkuk responds with: "Wait a minute. Your solution sounds worse than the problem!"

In the first complaint against God, he says, "The land is filled with violence!" And God seems to answer, "Don't worry. I'm bringing more violence. The violent will suffer violence."

Habakkuk says, "The land is filled with idolatry and wickedness and corruption." And God answers, "Don't worry. I'm bringing people who are more wicked, idolatrous, and corrupt to deal with them."

To this reply, Habakkuk raises a second complaint in verses 13–17: *"Why do you look idly at traitors? Why do you remain silent when the wicked swallow up the man more righteous than he?"* He's saying, "Yeah, we're not doing great, but those guys are worse! They are completely evil and wicked."

Part of the reason they're worse is that the Babylonians aren't just doing all of this wickedness. They are "rejoicing" over it (1:15). The description in 1:14–17 of the nets and dragnets was familiar imagery in the Ancient Near East. It conveyed the idea of conquerors grabbing people and roping them in, pulling them and dragging them, doing whatever they want with them as if they were gathering fish out of the lake. They are just hooking, pulling, and destroying them.

The Babylonians aren't noble warriors. They don't view themselves as people upholding justice and order in a world of chaos. The Babylonians were a ruthless nation rejoicing over the suffering that they were causing. They were plunderers who destroyed peoples, nations, and cultures.

Habakkuk is agreeing with God's assessment that these are guilty men whose own might is their strength (1:11), and it forms the basis of his second complaint: "Why would you use people like that? Their god is their own military power. They worship themselves. Are you gonna just let these people mercilessly kill forever?"

If God seemed uncaring in his silence, how much worse must this sort of reply have sounded to the man who had been crying out over and over for relief.

I'm guessing some of you have felt this way. Or perhaps even feel this way now.

Have you wrestled with the question of God's justice? Maybe as you've read through Scripture, you've read some of the accounts found there and thought, "How is that okay?"

God, how could you condone the conquest of Canaan? How could you be fine with the crazy things in the book of Judges or in the history of Israel? Or on a different level, how could you say that hell is the right response to sin? Eternal judgment? Eternal punishment? Really?

Have you wrestled with whether Biblical ethics are actually ethical? Have you ever found yourself in a place where you ask yourself the question, "If God is loving, then how come…?"

If so, then you understand some of the burden Habakkuk felt at God's answer. Habakkuk's struggle is that he thinks he knows how God is supposed to work, and then God says he's going to act in a very different way. We can relate. We think we know how a loving God ought to act, but then we see things happening that we can't reconcile with an all powerful God of love.

Sometimes the burden of God's silence is outweighed only by the burden of his answers. This can lead us into seasons of incredible struggle and doubt. If that's you, then maybe you can take comfort in the fact you're not alone. At the very least you have the prophet Habakkuk by your side. His prophecy is an expression of pained but faithful doubt.

———

Questions for Reflection

1. Have you ever been burdened by your experience of life in this world? Have you been burdened by the evil you see in the Christian church? What was the experience of this burden like for you?

2. In light of the question above, have you ever been like Habakkuk and felt like God is silent in the face of evil, especially the evil of those who claim to be his people? How did you experience the burden of God's silence?

3. Sometimes it isn't God's silence that burdens us but his clear declarations. Are there things God has said in Scripture, or specific answers the Bible gives to some of your questions, that you've found more troubling than God's silence?

4. How have you wrestled with these various burdens? Have you felt free to discuss them with God or within the community of a church? Where are you currently at with your faith? Emotionally? Intellectually? Spiritually?

---

1. Riad A. Kassis, *Frustrated with God: A Syrian Theologian's Reflections on Habakkuk,* (Riad A. Kassis, 2016), 9.

LESSONS FROM HABAKKUK'S
FAITHFUL DOUBT

Anyone who believes anything will automatically know something about doubt. But the person who knows why he believes is also in a position to discover why he doubts. The Christian should be such a person...

The world of Christian faith is not a fairy-tale, make-believe world, question-free and problem-proof, but a world where doubt is never far from faith's shoulder...

Consequently, a healthy understanding of doubt should go hand in hand with a healthy understanding of faith.

To insist that only doubt-free faith can be counted as genuine is to misunderstand what knowledge and faith are. The perfectionism in the demand is more destructive of genuine faith than the worst of doubts could ever be.

—Os Guinness, *Doubt: Faith In Two Minds*

Since the title of this book is *Faithful Doubt*, and since I've used that phrase a lot already, it may be helpful to stop at this point and consider more specifically what is meant by the phrase "faithful doubt" and what particular lessons about this we find in the book of Habakkuk. The lessons of faithful doubt are present throughout the book of Habakkuk, but it can be hard to name and process them. For that reason, I want us to press pause on the conversation between Habakkuk and God in order to list and discuss these lessons so that we have them in mind when we get back to the dialogue.

Lesson 1: There Is Such a Thing as Faithful Doubt

We need to begin by admitting that the expression "faithful doubt" can sound like an oxymoron to many people. Nevertheless, faithful doubt is what we see throughout the book of Habakkuk.

The words of Habakkuk are filled with frustration about God's apparent silence and indifference, as well as shock at the fact that God would use wicked and violent people to accomplish his purposes. To Habakkuk, the ways of this God he thought he knew seem dubious at best. Habakkuk is doubtful about what God is doing and saying.

And yet Habakkuk's faith is seen in what he does with his doubts, and the direction he chooses to move with them. In other words, it's actually the way he complains and expresses his doubts that demonstrates Habakkuk's faith to us.

Where does Habakkuk take his complaint? To whom does he go with his doubts about God's goodness? He goes straight to the source. He takes his anger, frustration, doubt, and shock to God.

This makes all the difference.

Think about this relationally. Suppose you have a friend who is upset with you about something. What is the difference of that friend complaining *to* you or *about* you? It's a big contrast, isn't it?

If I am just complaining *about* someone, then what I'm doing is really tearing her down and disparaging her to another person. If I'm saying everything I think and feel about that person to a third party, I'm effectively walking away from the relationship. I'm giving up and justifying my feelings about her without allowing her a chance to explain or respond. I've broken faith within the relationship and violated it. Simply complaining about someone is a prideful response largely geared toward justifying my own feelings and making myself feel vindicated in the situation.

However, complaining *to* someone can actually be a means of engagement. If I'm complaining to the person I'm allowing her a chance to speak and that enables her to give her side of the story and respond to my complaint. Complaining to her means actually engaging her and trying to figure out what's going on. It's an attempt to repair the relationship and move forward. It's also a demonstration of faith in the person.

Complaining to the person is an act of trust that, because of who she is, she must have some reasonable explanation for what I'm perceiving as a difficulty or problem. It shows her that I trust her enough to believe she might have something to say to address the concern. At the very least, by complaining to her instead of about her, I'm enabling the possibility of healing in the relationship and the possibility of moving forward into understanding.

Now, what is Habakkuk doing?

He's not complaining *about* God. He's complaining *to* him.

Despite his pain, anger, frustration, and doubts, he moves toward God with his issue. This is an act of faith. The essence of faith is trust, and Habakkuk trusts God will not reject him because of his doubt, and his questions, or even his anger at how God is operating. This doubtful complaining is indeed a relational action on Habakkuk's part.

You can see the relational nature of Habakkuk's complaints in the language he uses with God. In 1:2 he doesn't call him, "God" in a distance sense like referencing the blanket concept of the divine that's simply out there somewhere.

The capital letters of LORD in our English translations are the translator's way of transcribing the personal covenant name of God—Yahweh. As Habakkuk goes to God in his pain and frustration and anger, he's using his personal name: "Yahweh, help me understand what's going on here."

Habakkuk's use of personal pronouns helps us see the relational nature of this dialogue more clearly. In verse 1:12, he says, "Yahweh, *my* God, *my* Holy One." This God he is complaining to is his God, the one he knows. His questions and complaints come out of the relationship he already has with God. He's saying, "I understand that I am yours and you are mine." And if you look at the conclusion of Habakkuk's complaints in 2:1 how does he end? Habakkuk doesn't run off in a huff. He writes, *"I will take my stand at my watchpost and station myself on the tower, and look out to see what he will say to me, and what I will answer concerning my complaint."*

Habakkuk is saying, "I'm going to wait and see." He trusts that despite his doubt, because of who God is, there must be some sort of reply. There is some sort of answer to his complaints. Habakkuk is faithful and trusts God by assuming there is an answer to his complaints and that God will hear and respond. By going to him, he practices faith even in his doubts.

So the lesson for us is simple: there is such a thing as faithful doubt.

However, this raises some immediate questions for us:

What are we doing with our doubts and complaints about God and his ways?
Do you let your doubts and questions and frustrations about what God is or isn't doing provide you with an excuse to ignore and avoid God?
Or do your doubts, questions, and frustrations drive you to him?
Are you complaining to God or are you simply complaining about God?

Complaining to him is the way that doubt is expressed in faith. This leads us into the next lesson on faithful doubt.

Lesson 2: God Accepts and Even Condones Faithful Doubt.

It's important to notice that as Habakkuk brings his questions and complaints to God, he is received. God accepts his questions and even his frustrated anger. And there isn't even a hint of anger from God at these things.

This is the pattern we see throughout Scripture. Throughout the Bible, we encounter men and women expressing faithful doubt, and God always accepts their questions.

When we dig deeper though, there's even more to this. God doesn't just accept Habakkuk's questions. He condones them. To condone means to give approval, and part of the subtext of the book of Habakkuk is that God approves Habakkuk's questioning and complaining.

To see more clearly that God is condoning Habakkuk's faithful doubt we have to consider the nature of Scripture. As crazy as I know it sounds to many people, Christians believe that the Bible, the Scriptures of the Old and New Testament, are the actual inspired word of God. This means the Bible isn't a particular culture's take on God; it's God's take on God. The Bible isn't formed just from the opinion of its authors. It is God's opinion in print form.[1]

This belief doesn't just come out of thin air. In 2 Timothy 3:16 we're told, *"All Scripture is breathed out by God."* Second Peter 1:21 says, *"No prophecy was ever produced by the will of man, but men spoke from God as they were carried along by the Holy Spirit."* These passages teach us the understanding of the Bible just mentioned.

However, it's very possible, maybe even likely, that as you read this book you're not at a place where you believe the Bible is the literal word of God breathed out by him and written by people carried along by the Holy Spirit. If that's you, I totally get it.

For the sake of argument though, let's assume it's true. After all, if the Bible isn't the word of God, then the book of Habakkuk is quite possibly just the ravings of an ancient eccentric, so why should you care what he has to teach you? So for now let's assume the Bible is the inspired word of God—his authoritative take on life, the universe, and everything, including himself.

Now let's connect the dots.

What is the book of Habakkuk? It's Scripture, which according to 2 Timothy 3:16 means Habakkuk was breathed out by God.

Habakkuk is also a book of prophecy, which according to 2 Peter 1:21 means that in this book we have a record of the prophet speaking from God as he was carried along by the Holy Spirit. We see something of this in Habakkuk's own description of his book. In verse 1:1 he starts by saying this writing is an *oracle that Habakkuk the prophet saw."*

Habakkuk is stating that while the whole of the book are his words, they're words given to him by God. When we connect all these dots, it tells us the questioning and the complaining against God we see in Habakkuk is actually inspired by God.

Think about that for a moment.

The Spirit of God inspired these questions directed against God's very character. According to 2 Peter, the

Holy Spirit is the one who carried Habakkuk along in his complaining to God. According to 2 Timothy 3:16, God breathed out these words of faithful doubt through Habakkuk. The Holy Spirit is the one who led Habakkuk not to simply utter these words but to write them down and record them. Furthermore, the Holy Spirit has continued working throughout history ensuring that these words would be preserved and transmitted down to this very day in order that we might come to know God through them.

If that's true, then it means God is showing us he doesn't just accept our questions and our doubts—he condones them. In fact, I think he's showing us that, given the state of the world, we should have them. Through the faithful doubt of Habakkuk, God is teaching you that if you have an actual trust in the fact that God is good then you should have some questions.

In other words, if you can look at the state of this world and not be troubled, not be frustrated, not be angry even at God's apparent inaction and indifference, then the message of God through Habakkuk is that there is actually something wrong with your faith. If you aren't greatly bothered by the evil all around and within you, maybe you don't truly believe that God is good and desires something better for you and the world. The fact that God condones faithful doubt means it's not simply something you *may* have. It's something you *should* have.

However, with that in mind, we need to consider the third lesson of faithful doubt.

Lesson 3: Practicing Faithful Doubt Might Not Bring You the Answers You Want

God accepts and condones faithful doubt. He encourages us to come to him with our doubts and questions and to be honest with him about them.

However, nowhere does he promise to give us answers or that the answers he does give will be ones we want to hear. God responds to Habakkuk's faithful doubts and questions but not in the way Habakkuk had hoped he would.

We will see this more clearly in the next chapter, but we've already discussed that while God gives Habakkuk answers, those same answers leave the prophet shocked and horrified. Habakkuk thinks he knows how God should operate. He has expectations for how God should answer these questions, and God blows Habakkuk's expectations out of the water.

This is a lesson we must keep in mind. It's important for you to know that you can go to God with all of your questions, doubts, and frustrations. You can even go to him when you're angry at him. He will not reject you, but he doesn't promise you will like what he has to say. He doesn't even guarantee you'll be able to comprehend the answers he gives you or that you'll understand why he doesn't give you all the answers you may want.

God clearly tells us his thoughts are not our thoughts, and his ways are not our ways (Is. 55:8). And that his judgments are unsearchable and his ways are inscrutable to us (Ro. 11:33).

This should be a no-brainer for those of us who believe

the biblical teaching on God's nature. If God is infinite and eternal, there is no way we can fully comprehend him. And because of that, we might not be able to comprehend all he allows to come to pass.

Even though it should be a no-brainer, this is not an easy thing to accept, and it's probably not a comforting thing to hear. Particularly if you are currently experiencing deep pain from living in this broken world. However, I want to suggest that it's actually a good thing. Let me try to give you two brief reasons why it may be good that you might not get the answers you want from God.

First, if you find God's words and his ways difficult, it might be an indication that you're dealing with the real God. In *The Reason for God*, pastor Tim Keller references a helpful illustration based on the old movie *The Stepford Wives*.

The movie is built around the concept of a group of men who've turned their wives into robots, people who just say "Yes," smile, and do what their husbands want. Their wives now live to serve them, to appease their every need.

Keller points out that while the men in the story may think this is amazing, it means there's no real relationship with their wives. Everything in the relationship is fake. The husbands have just created automatons to do their bidding.

Perhaps you already see where Keller is going with this. We can tend to do the same thing with God. Keller writes, "Only if your God can say things that outrage you and make you struggle, as in a real friendship or marriage, only then will you know that you have gotten hold of a real God and not a figment of your imagination."[2]

The fact that the God of the Bible might perplex you; the fact that the God of the Bible might not agree with your ethics or he might not agree with your moral code—might be an indication that he is beyond your culture and bigger than your experience and your world. And therefore, maybe he is the real God.

This leads to the second reason many have suggested that God's answers not being what we want is actually a good thing.

Let me put it to you with these questions:

Do you really want a God who doesn't have purposes that you can't understand?

Do you really want a God who is limited to interacting with the world on the basis of your perspective?

If your god never disagrees with you, then it might just be your own spiritual projection or imagination. If you have a god that cannot have purposes or answers beyond your small experience of the world and of time itself, well that's not much of a god. If God is limited to what I can see and what I can understand and by my intelligence, then he is not really worth trusting.

It's precisely because he knows more than we do—because he has a bigger picture and a greater perspective —that we can trust in God even as we struggle with him. And it's precisely because he is this bigger God—immortal, eternal, all-powerful, and all-knowing—that he is not troubled by our doubts and questions.

The good news is that we are not just left here with this God. We're not just called to blindly trust this God, and that takes us to the last lesson of faithful doubt.

Lesson 4: Practicing Faithful Doubt Doesn't Remove Pain, But It Puts It into Context

Remember the first lesson we talked about. Habakkuk isn't complaining *about* God. He's complaining *to* him. He is being faithful with his doubts and questions by taking them to God. He goes to God with his complaints and frustrations and cries out to him in his pain.

By his faithful trust in God, he is pursuing relationship with God even with his complaints. Even in his complaining, it's still all about relationship. Bible scholar James Bruckner summarizes the issue this way:

> Questions and lament are part of a believer's burden, and honest dialogue with God is a necessary form of relationship with him....
>
> Habakkuk's protest is faithful and inspired because it is done out of the conviction that God is good all the time, even in death and dying. This conviction does not silence the questions and pain of the faithful in Scripture. Rather, it focuses the questions in the form of personal dialogue with a loving Creator and Redeemer, who accompanies the sufferer and will, in perfect time, bring victory, healing, and restoration. Those who long for the

kingdom of God with its peace, love, and goodness may find hope on the pathway of lament and faithful protest.[3]

Bruckner is saying Habakkuk can be faithful with his doubts precisely because he knows who this God is. Habakkuk is calling out to God on the basis of his personal knowledge of what God has done in ages past. He trusts God has reasons for how he's acting because he trusts that God is good. He calls him, "My Lord" and "My Holy One" because he is in relationship with him. Habakkuk trusts that God is good not because of abstract doctrinal supposition, but because he has a history with him.

There's more though. His relationship gives Habakkuk confidence precisely because of what he knows about this God. In 1:12 Habakkuk calls God "everlasting," and this gives him a faint glimmer of hope. Since God is everlasting, Habakkuk trusts that his people will somehow remain. They shall live.

This confidence and trust in God's nature leads Habakkuk to engage with him despite distress. Once he remembers who God is—the Everlasting One, My Lord, My Holy One—what does he say? *"We will not die."*

Habakkuk is saying, "I don't understand. I can't put everything in its proper place, but I know who *you* are, and therefore I know that we will not die. Somehow your people will continue. Somehow your people will have a place, even though you just told me you are bringing destruction. You just told me the Babylonians are going to wipe us out like the Assyrians wiped out Israel. But we will not die. Just like you, your promises are everlasting, so your promises to us will remain."

In this verse Habakkuk also calls God his "rock." A rock is something strong and unmovable. It's a source of stability. This is a common description of God throughout the Bible.

God is one in whom we can take refuge. He is the one who can give us stability because he is immovable. For those who know him, God is a rock, and his people can rest in his secure strength.

In Habakkuk 3, the prophet will show us that his confidence comes because of how God has worked in the past. He had proved his fatherly love and care to his people time and time again. It's because of this that, in the midst of his confusion and pain, Habakkuk trusts this God. He knows who God is and all that he has done for his people. Habakkuk is confused and frustrated by his current circumstances but his knowledge of who God is enables him to move toward him in faith despite his doubts. And his knowledge of who this God is makes the pain of his frustration and doubt more bearable.

I have a repeated conversation with my children that boils down to my identity. My kids will get a scrape or a cut, and I have to clean the wound.

It hurts, and they know it's going to hurt. One of them tends to freak out whenever this situation arises, and I have to speak words of comfort to her. I don't say, "This won't hurt" because that's a lie. I don't say, "Okay, I won't do it" because I have to do it. But, I ask questions.

Me: Do I love you?

Her: Yes.

Me: Do you think I want to hurt you?

Her: No

Me: Do you know I'm trying to help you?

Her: Yes.

Me: Then trust me.

When I have to discipline my kids, similar questions often get asked.

Me: Do you think I'm doing this because I don't like you?

Them: No.

Me: Do you think I'm doing this because I want to be mean to you?

Them: No.

Me: Then why am I doing this?

Them: (begrudging and sulking) Because you love me.

Me: Then trust me.

As my kids have gotten older, they have more questions about why they're not allowed to do certain things. They wonder why we limit their screen time and online activities. They don't understand our "No sleepovers" policy. Their relationship with me as their father doesn't remove the pain of difficult circumstances, or the pain of not understanding all of my reasoning or purposes but their knowledge that I really do love and care for them, that I am working for their good—well that can put the pain, frustration, and difficulty into a new light. At least when they actually remember these things. The same is true of our relationship with God.

I know it's cliché, but this truth always makes me think of the over-quoted words of C.S. Lewis in *The Lion, the Witch, and the Wardrobe*. Lucy and Susan are wrestling over the fact that Aslan is a lion and they ask, "Is he safe?" Mr. Beaver gives a wise, biblical response, one that summarizes this lesson from Habakkuk about faithful doubt. He responds with a smirk: Are you crazy? He's a lion. Mr. Beaver says, "Who said anything about safe? 'Course he isn't safe. But he's good. He's the king, I tell you."[4]

God is not safe, and he's not comfortable. But when you truly know him and all he's done for you, it does bring comfort because it proves that he is good. Knowing who God is and all he has done puts the pain and frustration and anger we might have at him into a context where we find those things easier to endure. We can accept struggle and doubt because we remember that, while he may not comfort us with the words we want, he will give us the ultimate comfort and help we need. While he may not be safe in the way that we want, he is good.

Those of us who live in the shadow of the cross have even more reason than Habakkuk to trust that whatever comes to pass is because he is good. God loves us so much, he cares so much, that he came himself and became a man to suffer with us and for us. In the person of Jesus, God takes on flesh. He becomes one of us, entering our darkness.

To use the language of Habakkuk, the wicked surrounded Christ, the righteous one. Justice for him was paralyzed. He suffers violence, strife, contention, and destruction for us to save us from them. He becomes one of the fish caught in the net of the wicked in order to burst it apart and bring you freedom.

This doesn't remove all of my questions or all of my doubts, but knowing what God has done for me in Jesus enables me to better accept whatever he allows to happen to me. Knowing what Jesus has done for you can help you to accept whatever he allows to come to pass in your life.

Not without pain. Not without questions. Not without frustration. But when you know more of who this God is and all he's done you can cry out in faithful doubt that he is your Lord. He is your Holy One. He is your Rock. You will not die.

Questions for Reflection

1. What are your thoughts on the concept of "faithful doubt"? Does this change your understanding of what it means to have questions or doubts? Why or why not?

2. What do you think of the idea that God doesn't just accept faithful doubt, he condones it? How does this change your understanding of what it means to wrestle with doubts?

3. What do you think about the statement that if you don't have any doubts something might be wrong with your faith?

4. Are there particular answers in Scripture you understand to be true but struggle with like Habakkuk did?

5. How can personal relationship with God help put our difficulties into context? Have you found this to be true personally? If so, how or when?

6. How does knowledge of the cross influence your understanding of what it means to trust God in the face of pain and suffering.

7. Can you say that you know this God we are talking about? How do you know you know him?

---

1. The understanding of the inspiration and authority of Scripture is a key tenet of Christian belief. And yet there has been a lot of debate on what the best words are to describe this—inspired, inerrant, infallible, etc. There is much history and nuance around this debate but at the end of the day the simplest way to put is that the Bible is not a word about God, it is ultimately a word from God himself. For one of the more concise explanations of what is and is not meant by this check out the *Chicago Statement on Biblical Inerrancy*: https://www.etsjets.org/files/documents/Chicago_Statement.pdf

2. Timothy Keller, *The Reason for God: Belief in an Age of Skepticism*, (New York: Dutton, 2008), 114.

3. James Bruckner, *The NIV Application Commentary: Jonah, Nahum, Habakkuk, Zephaniah* (Grand Rapids: Zondervan, 2004), 214, 215.

4. C.S. Lewis, *The Lion, the Witch, and the Wardrobe* (New York: Harper-Collins, 1978), 86.

EVIL, JUDGMENT, AND GRACE

HABAKKUK 1:1–2:20

The Bible simply doesn't appear to want to say what God can say about evil. That provides a powerful extra argument for the point... that at least one tradition within Christian thought has warned against our trying to explain it at all.

—N. T. Wright, *Evil and the Justice of God*

In the first chapter, we talked about how Habakkuk is burdened by everything he sees around him, but more importantly he's burdened by what he thinks God isn't doing. His prophesy is constructed around two complaints. The first one concerns the wickedness of God's people and how Judah, the Southern Kingdom centered in Jerusalem, looked just like the surrounding pagan nations. Judah is filled with violence, wickedness, and perversion of justice. Yet God seems idle and indifferent to all of that.

God then replies to Habakkuk saying he isn't idle, and in fact he's bringing the Babylonians to judge and punish his wicked people. Habakkuk hears this, and it burdens him even more. He says, "Wait a minute! Those guys are worse than we are!" That's why his complaint goes out that *"the wicked swallow up the ones more righteous than him."* Again, the complaint is centered around the questions:

Why are you idle?
Why don't you do something?
Why don't you act the way I expect you to?

That's the basic context of this prophecy. As we continue to consider the teaching of Habakkuk and its implications for us, I want to look at three connected but distinct issues related to these questions: The Burdensome Problem of Evil, the Silencing Answer of Judgment, and The Costly Hope of Grace.

The Burdensome Problem of Evil

The problem of evil is a theological dilemma that has been discussed and debated for millennia. All that debate and discussion can be summed up with a question: How is there evil in the world if God is both all powerful and all good?

If God is all good, then he should desire there be no evil in the world. And if he is all powerful, he should have the ability to prevent or remove that evil. However, there obviously is evil in the world. So what's up? Is God just not powerful enough to deal with what he hates and therefore he can't remove it? Or is he powerful enough to remove it, but maybe just not as good as he says he is which is why he doesn't do anything?

There is a lot more to the problem of evil, but the heart of the issue lies in these questions. If you reconsider Habakkuk's complaints, you see this is precisely what he's wrestling with. Why isn't God doing something about that rampant evil around him? How could he use the rampant evil of the Babylonians? How is this the behavior of a good God?

As we discussed in the last chapter, Habakkuk is coming from a place of faith not skepticism with these questions. He believes in God's power and his goodness. In fact, this is precisely why he has these questions. Habakkuk makes the declaration that God is of purer eyes than to even see evil. He writes, *"You cannot look at wrong"* (2:13).

What's he assuming here? That God is good, perfectly good. Habakkuk assumes God is perfectly pure. He can't even look upon evil. And yet at the same time, as Habakkuk notes in 1:3 and again in 2:13, God seems idle in the face of it all. Habakkuk thinks he is idly looking at traitorous, treacherous evil and remaining silent! Again, though, what is Habakkuk assuming? He's assuming that God does in fact have the power and ability to address evil, but he simply isn't doing so.

The "idling" language here highlights his frustration. Consider the power of an idling car. It has the power to move. It just needs to be put into gear. In a sense, what Habakkuk is asking God here is:

God, when are you going put it in gear?

Why aren't you moving?

Why aren't you doing something here?

Habakkuk's faith and trust in who God is and what he is able to do causes him to be burdened by all of this. It's because he believes God is good and because he believes God is powerful, he finds the realities of evil and oppression and wickedness so burdensome. Paradoxically, it's the faith of Habakkuk that makes him go even deeper in his doubts and uncertainties and the questions stemming from them.

Habakkuk goes deeper in his questioning when he makes reference to God as the Creator of mankind in 1:14. When he does this he is pushing past the question of "Why don't you do something about this situation?" to the more serious question of "How did we even get to this point? You made all mankind. You made all mankind like fish, and you made others like those who pull fish up and tear them apart. C'mon God, why do the wicked exist at all?" Habakkuk is wrestling with the burdensome problem of evil.

Habakkuk shows us these are not just the questions of the unbeliever and the skeptical. Furthermore, the presence of these sorts of questions here in Habakkuk and throughout Scripture show us these are not just questions faithful people *may* have. They are questions faithful people *should* have.[1] If I believe that God is all powerful and all good, I should find the presence and reality of evil burdensome and problematic.

The same is true today. If God is all powerful and all good, why are there approximately around 20.9 million global victims of human trafficking? If God is all good and all powerful, then why are there 600,000 to 800,000 people, half of whom are children, every year who are bought and sold as slaves for forced labor or commercial sex? If God is all powerful and all good, why is it that the Syrian war continues raging and has left over 400,000 people dead? If God is all good, and he's all powerful, why does ISIS exist? Why is Boko Haram allowed to continue their regime of torture, rape, enslavement, and murder? What about the many other murderous groups we don't even hear about because it doesn't concern our nation's political interest? And what about the wickedness of that?

If God is all powerful and all good, and he thinks family is important, why do countless parents face the decision of either staying in dangerous and economically deprived situations or risking a border crossing with their children? Why are many of those families ripped apart at the US border?

If God is all powerful and all good, why is it that around 90,000 Christians are killed for their faith every year? And why is it that so many Western Christians don't really think about this? How could God allow the apathy of Christians to the killing of their brothers and sisters?

These aren't questions we tend to talk about in church, but they should be. These questions are all throughout Scripture. The reality of evil is never softened in the Bible. It's never minimized or played down. The questions I've asked here are just the tip of the iceberg when it comes to the presence and reality of evil in this world. If we take these seriously then, like Habakkuk, we should cry out, *"Why are you silent, O God? Why are you idle?*

Why does evil exist at all?" These are questions the faithful should have.

These questions are accepted and even encouraged throughout Scripture. At the same time, Scripture never resolves the problem of evil. God doesn't give a full explanation of this problem in the book of Habakkuk or anywhere else. He makes no attempt to defend himself. He also makes no attempt to satisfy all of our questions. Scripture does, however, give us some boundaries as we wrestle with this problem of evil.

It speaks of God being holy and perfectly good. It speaks of him being completely powerful and sovereign. It talks about human responsibility and all sorts of pertinent things. Yet, it never gives a solution. It never says all we want it to at this point. New Testament scholar N. T. Wright summarizes:

> Somehow, strangely (and to us sometimes even annoyingly), the Creator God will not simply abolish evil from his world. The question that swirls around in these discussions is, Why not? We are not given an answer; we are instead informed in no uncertain terms that God will contain evil, that he will restrain it, that he will prevent it from doing its worst, and that he will even on occasion use the malice of human beings to further his own strange purposes.[2]

God contains evil. He restrains it. He will prevent it from doing its worst. He will even subvert it to his own ends. Those are boundary points, but the problem isn't resolved. There's no logical explanation given.

I think the reason for this, at least in part, is because it's inappropriate to do so. The Bible portrays evil as an intruder in this world. It's something that doesn't belong. And in some sense, trying to find a fully satisfying explanation to the problem of evil is an attempt to rationalize its existence and make a place for it in this world where it has no rightful place. God won't rationalize evil because it doesn't make sense. Evil is folly. And God will not dignify it with a rationale and reason for existing in this world. It simply doesn't belong.

However, while God doesn't give an explanation for evil he does have one particular answer for Habakkuk and us.

The Silencing Answer of Judgment

Throughout the book of Habakkuk, we see God stating that evil will not stand. He clearly and repeatedly communicates that evil is going to be judged and punished. When Habakkuk brings his first complaint about the wickedness and the corruption of the people of God in Judah, God says, "Yes, and judgment is going to come upon them for their wickedness and for their evil." Then when Habakkuk doesn't like that answer, he says, "But the Babylonians are worse than we are. They are more wicked and they are more corrupt." God says, "Yes, and they will be punished as well. They will also face judgment according to their sin."

The concept of divine judgment is not something we're comfortable with. Modern Westerners in particular find the idea of judgment to be unpalatable. It seems harsh

and maybe even barbaric to us, something from an unen-
lightened age. However, there are a few things we should
notice about these judgments.

First, the judgment talked about here in Habakkuk is
just and appropriate to the offenses. Consider how apt
and fitting these judgments are. When the people of God,
who are supposed to reflect God and his ways into the
world, become just like the pagan nations around them
God gives them up to the pagan nations around them. In
essence, it's as if God has said, "You have become more
like them than like me, so I will give you to them and let
them deal with you." It's a punishment that fits the crime.

Then the wickedness of the Babylonians is described as
them being puffed up or swollen with their pride and arrogance. They are puffed and swollen with their thoughts
that they are the kings of their own destiny. In his judgments against them, God says he is going to deflate them.
He will remove their pride from them and return them to
an appropriate size. Again, their judgment is fitting.

Furthermore, the future judgment of Babylon is
described in a series of five woes. In the Bible, a woe is a
word of judgment or a declaration of coming affliction on
someone due to their own actions. The five woes
addressed to Babylon are very fitting. Consider the
following:

1st Woe—2:6b–8: The plunderers shall be
plunderers.

2nd Woe—2:9–11: They built a house (legacy) on
blood and violence, so by blood and violence it will

be forfeited. In fact, the very house they built cries out against them.

3rd Woe—2:12–14: They built a city of iniquity by blood (violence) to boast of their strength so through violence it will disappear. Their city of iniquity built to bring them fame and renown will come to nothing and be forgotten while knowledge of the God they thought they defeated will cover the earth.

4th Woe—2:15–18: They made other nations drink a cup of wrath and stripped them naked exposing and shaming them in their weakness. God will make the Babylonians drink the cup of his wrath and strip them of their strength shaming them before the nations they shamed.

5th Woe—2:18–20: Their idolatry, which is ultimately a trust in themselves and their own strength will be revealed for the folly it is. The punishment here is that God will let them depend on their gods. These are gods who can do nothing for them, gods who truly are silent, who can't speak, and what the true God is going to reveal to them is that their strength is nothing compared to his. Their gods are dead, lifeless things. Their temples are empty. His temple is filled with his presence. God is alive, he is active, he will speak and work against them.

What's more fitting is the method of delivery for these

woes. In 2:6, we see that all the peoples the Babylonians ruined are being gathered together to speak these woes over them. It's like the ultimate victim impact statement. God is bringing Babylon's victims to help declare justice and judgment over them. What we see here again is that the punishments fit the crime. God is showing Habakkuk that he is just. He is paying attention. He does see. He is not idle.

It should be noted that all of these woes came to pass. Judah falls to the Babylonians around 587 BC. Then the Babylonians fall to the Persians in 539 BC.

The second thing to notice about the judgments of God in Habakkuk is the fact that they silence all the questions. God is enacting these judgments because they are right, and they are good, but they also bring a fitting conclusion to the conversation in the book. This dialogue starts with Habakkuk's complaints and questions about God's silence. It ends with Habakkuk's silence. He doesn't have any more questions.

Throughout chapters 1 and 2, there is a ton of irony, and we see it come to a sharp point in these judgments. Judah becomes like the pagans, so to the pagans they go. In all these woes there's an ironic justice—the plunderers are plundered, the violent come to a violent end, and so forth. There's more though.

The silence of God is a significant theme throughout chapters 1 and 2 of the book. The prophet's two complaints are centered on God's apparent idleness and silence. The big question in the face of evil: Why doesn't God say something?

In contrast, Habakkuk isn't silent. He's speaking out in

concern over God's silence, and he's waiting for an answer. In 2:13 you see that this is his very question: "Why are you silent?" Even in the woes, we see a parallel of this irony about silence. The Babylonians go to their silent stone, their silent idols who cannot answer them. Then in 2:20, we get the final nail in the coffin of the judgment leveled against the Babylonians: *"God, the LORD, is in his holy temple. Let all the earth keep silence before him."* There is a play on words here. Despite what Habakkuk might think of God's silence, and despite what the wicked nations think of this silent God (and thinking they can do anything to his people because of his silence), when God shows up he is not idle or silent. In fact, when he speaks everyone else is silenced.

To go back a bit though, it's important to note that the reasoning of the Babylonians makes sense. If God truly were silent, if he really was idle, then might does make right. They should trust in their strength. They should exploit the weak. They should do whatever they want because they are the masters of their own destiny.

But the Babylonians are wrong. As is often the case, those who are committed to their evil fail to take God into account, and these woes and judgments reveal the folly of evil for what it is.

When we get to Habakkuk 3, we'll see Habakkuk has some more to say, but he has no more questions. No more complaints. It's as if Habakkuk is saying, "I don't fully understand, but I have nothing else that I can say against you. You have silenced me, so I will simply trust you."

Since God is in his holy temple, evil will not have the final word. God speaks, and the boasts of evil are silenced.

What God is telling us through the promise of a true judgment is that he does see. Furthermore, his answer of judgment does many things, but key among them is that it exposes our hypocrisy. God's judgment of evil still acts in this way to silence many of our questions.

Culturally and generationally, many of us are content to accuse God of being idle and silent. We look at the evil of the world and say, "Well, why does God allow that to happen? Why doesn't he do something?" There's a cultural arrogance to this where we feel free to judge God for his inaction, and then judge him again for how he promises to act in the future. This is where we see the inconsistency and hypocrisy that often lies unchecked in our heart. We accuse God of doing nothing, and then in Scripture when he shows us that he is going to do something, we accuse him of being harsh, ungracious, unloving.

We're a culture that wants to hear nothing about judgment. If I gave people advance warning that I was preaching a sermon on the judgment of sin, the response of many would be, "Oh no! We don't want to sit through that." We think of such messages as fire and brimstone preaching, and we write them off as primitive fundamentalism. We think we don't need to hear all that sort of stuff. It's unhelpful for outreach or for comforting people. Indeed, we think it could be psychologically damaging to talk about judgment.

Yet might it be, like with Habakkuk, that God sees better than we do? When it comes to his promise to judge evil in this life and the in the next—might that not silence us by showing us he is actually more serious about the problem of evil than we are? The overwhelming message of the Bible is that God takes it more seriously than we can imagine, and he will ultimately bring judgment to bear on all evil.

He is the God who hears. He hears every cry of every victim, every second of every day. He is the God who is all powerful and everywhere present, which means he sees and experiences every single injustice, every single oppression, every single act of violence and abuse, every instance of suffering. We see a bare snippet of the true evil of the world, and we presume to judge him for promising judgment. However, if we saw like he does, we might not think his words of judgment were harsh. We might not think them barbaric, disproportionate, or unfair.

In our dislike of judgment, we also create a false dichotomy. When we hear of God's judgment, we tend to think, "That's the Old Testament God. That Old Testament God is full of wrath and judging and whatnot, but the New Testament God is a God of love and grace."

This is a false dichotomy because there is just as much love and grace of God in the Old Testament as the New. And there's just as much, if not more, about God's judgment and wrath in the New.

The New Testament tells us of Jesus who is meek and mild. Sure. It tells us Jesus came to serve and save. Yes. But the New Testament is also clear in its proclamation of Jesus as the King, Lord, and Judge of the universe. In Scripture, it is Jesus who actually has the most explicit things to say about the judgment and punishment of eternal death in hell, and Jesus who says the wicked will not escape it (Matthew 10:28, 13:40–43, 22:13, 25:41; Mark 9:43; Luke 12:5; etc.).

What's more, Jesus is the one who actually intensifies the problem of evil for us by saying it's not a problem "out there." He highlights the truth that the problem of evil is not merely an abstract philosophical dilemma to be debated, but a reality inside of us that needs to be dealt with. He does this by highlighting the root of evil. It's not just murder that is a problem; it's anger (Matthew 5:21–22). It's not just adultery but every lustful thought (Matthew 5:27–30). He intensifies the problem of evil and shows that it's *our* problem. Jesus tells us evil is something that lies in every human heart, including yours and mine.

Of course this raises concerns for us, and maybe that's partly why we don't like thinking about the judgment of God. If we thought consistently about Jesus' words, we would have to acknowledge that judgment might fall on us. As a Christian pastor, I'm not really like the Babylonians described in Habakkuk. However, if I'm honest I have to admit I might look more like Judah, the people who should know God and resemble him yet who were apathetic when it came to issues of justice and the poor, whom they were oppressing. Maybe much of the American church looks more like Judah in its adherence to the heresy of the Prosperity Gospel and hiring false prophets to say what we want to hear and have our spiritual ears tickled, or looking to politicians on the left or the right to save us. Why should we not see this as part of the problem of evil needing judgment?

You might be more Babylonian or more Judean in your

evil, but a close examination of your heart reveals clearly that the problem of evil and the need for judgment starts right there—in your own life. The problem of evil isn't something that just lies out there in the world. The problem of evil lies in every single one of our hearts.

And God promises to judge evil, all of it. He will judge the evil we see which causes us distress as well as the evil we find it more convenient to gloss over and dismiss. When he speaks his final and ultimate word of judgment on evil the whole world will be silent. This would be an unbearable reality to consider if it weren't for the fact that Habakkuk also points us to the costly hope of grace.

The Costly Hope of Grace

Anyone even remotely familiar with the message of Christianity knows that it speaks of forgiveness, mercy, salvation, and the assurance of grace. We believe in the forgiveness of our evil and the removal of sins. And yet, for many this seems to flaunt the idea of judgment and justice we just discussed. I sympathize with my non-believing friends who say, "You know what? That kinda sounds like a cop out to me. You're telling me the guilt of a sex offender can just be wiped out, all his sins forgiven? You're telling me that the murderer on his death bed can simply turn to God, and everything's ok? I don't want that God. There's no justice in that. That's cheap grace."

I understand this concern, and I think many in the church can end up portraying grace that is cheap. That is why we have to remember the hope of grace is actually costly.

The Gospel isn't about God ignoring our evil. The Gospel is not about God ignoring injustice. The Gospel is about God bearing his own judgment for our evil. The Gospel says God made Christ to be sin for us. He doesn't overlook our sin. He doesn't pretend our evil doesn't exist. He came to bear the full penalty and judgment of evil in himself (2 Corinthians 5:21).

The promise of grace is this: Jesus is plundered for us plunderers. Violence comes upon him as he receives the violence due to us. He comes to nothing because of our iniquity. He receives the cup of wrath we should have swallowed.[3] He's stripped naked on the cross and exposed to the ridicule, scorn, and shame that was and is due to us.

Jesus is ultimately the one who cries out, *"Father, why have you forsaken me?"* (Mark 15:34). Which is a question similar to, "Why are you idle?" And Jesus receives the same silence of God that distressed Habakkuk. This is the Gospel. Grace is free to us, but it cost Jesus everything. God brings justice to every single sin. If you are forgiven, it is because Jesus was judged for you. He was destroyed for you. That might sound harsh, but it's the clear message of Scripture (Isaiah 53:10–11). And it's incredibly important to remember.

Consider this question: Why did the nation of Judah go so far astray? The evidence of Scripture shows that it was because they were presumptuous about grace. They thought about their identity as the ones God had brought out of Egypt and established as a nation. They proudly looked at his redemptive work on their behalf and became complacent about their own evil. They forgot about God's judgment. They ignored his warnings, and it led them into arrogance and wickedness, resulting in Habakkuk's first complaint (1:2–4) about God's people. It was their understanding of salvation that led them to abuse grace and cheapen it.

The Christian church is prone to this same dangerous complacency. We should rest in grace and find comfort, hope, and confidence in grace, yet we must take the cost of that grace seriously so that we never take it lightly. As a pastor, it terrifies me when someone claims Christianity but thinks nothing of his or her personal evil. Far too many people call themselves by the name of Christ and then take sin lightly or minimize that for which he had to die in order to forgive them. That is a dangerous place to be.

The New Testament is full of the same types of warnings that went to God's people in the Old Testament. The Apostle Paul says if you claim Christ yet continue in a blatant lifestyle of sin as if grace was cheap and easy— then you are grieving the Holy Spirit (Ephesians 4:30). The author of Hebrews puts it even more starkly, saying that if you take this grace lightly and continue to sin as if it didn't matter—you are trampling the blood of Christ (Hebrews 10:29). And Jesus, who is our gracious and loving Lord, says if you ignore the cost of grace, if you don't take it seriously—he will *"spit you out of his mouth"* (Revelation 3:16). We have to think about the cost of grace, so we don't take it for granted, and so we have a right response to Jesus.

This all means there is no such thing as cheap grace. Grace cost God his Son. Grace cost Jesus the suffering of the full wrath of God's judgment. God doesn't ignore evil —not the evil out there in the world nor the evil in every one of our hearts. Grace doesn't mean getting away with evil. It means having evil accounted for and dealt with more fully than we can even imagine. Grace comes at a cost, but it's a cost Jesus paid. And because Jesus has paid this cost, we can have hope in his grace. We can take both the cost of our forgiveness and the hope of grace seriously.

In Luke 7, Jesus is at a dinner party with a bunch of religious leaders, people who thought they were doing okay morally and spiritually. All of a sudden a notoriously sinful woman comes in and begins to anoint Jesus' feet and to weep over them. All the other guests look at her with scorn and derision, but Jesus tells a story. He says, *"Answer me this: a money lender forgave debts. One guy had a few debts, and one guy had great debt. Which one of these people will love the money lender more?"* The Pharisee says, *"Well I suppose the one with the greater debt."* And Jesus says, *"You're right."* He goes on to say, *"Those who are forgiven little love little. Those who are forgiven much love much."* What he is saying to the Pharisee is not that he has little to be forgiven of, but that he didn't take seriously the cost of his forgiveness. But the woman did. In light of the cost of her forgiveness, she rejoiced. She wept. She had joy. It changed her life.

If you understand the problem of evil is not just a problem out there in the world but a problem with your own heart, you'll be more in touch with the reality of the situation. And the more you understand the depth and breadth of the problem of evil, the more you will recognize that God's judgment is just. The more you realize all of this, the more you will be moved with gratitude and joy because you will realize how much you really needed to be forgiven for your evil and just what that forgiveness has cost. This realization will make you love him more even when you do struggle with doubts about his ways and his apparent silence in the face of evil. This realization will also turn your presumption into gratitude.

The God of the Bible is not aloof and indifferent to your suffering or the suffering of the world. In Jesus, he entered fully into it and bore the weight of the evil and suffering of the world upon himself in order to free sufferers from their burden and bring them into the comfort of his salvation.

———

Questions for Reflection

1. How have you heard the problem of evil discussed by those inside and outside the church? Have you struggled personally with the problem of evil?
2. What do you think about the fact that no logical rational explanation is given in Scripture for the problem of evil? How do you feel about the suggestion that it may actually be inappropriate to try to give such an answer?
3. What are your thoughts on the suggestion that our aversion to talking or hearing about God's

judgment might reveal a hypocrisy in us? Do you agree or disagree that his promise to judge sin in this life and in the next might silence us by showing us God is actually more serious about the problem of evil than we are?

4. Jesus' discussion of sin intensifies the problem of evil by showing it isn't a problem that lies outside of us. Evil lies in every single one of our hearts, meaning our hearts themselves need to be judged. What do you think about this? How does it make you feel?

5. Discuss the difference between "cheap grace" and the Gospel. How does the teaching that the Gospel is not about God ignoring injustice, but rather about God bearing his own judgment for our evil affect your understanding of what Christ has done for you?

---

1. See Lesson 2 in the previous chapter.
2. Wright, *Evil and the Justice of God*, 45, 55.
3. Compare Habakkuk 2:16; Isaiah 51:17; and Jeremiah 25:15 with Matthew 26:39.

A SONG OF FAITH
HABAKKUK 3:1-19

Habakkuk resolves to be joyful, not superficially with eyes closed to the struggle for justice or deliverance but looking truth in the face.
—James Bruckner, *Jonah, Nahum, Habakkuk, Zephaniah*

While you're doing fine, there's some people and I
Who have a really tough time getting through this life
So excuse us while we sing to the sky
—twentyonepilots, *Screen*

Imagine you are witnessing an intense disagreement between close friends. They argue back and forth, and one friend becomes heated in his remarks, making serious accusations about the character of the other. During all this, the other friend remains relatively calm yet firm as he challenges the veracity of his friend's assumptions. Then all of a sudden in the middle of this argument, the friend who has been angry and agitated spontaneously bursts into a song celebrating how faithful a friend the other man had always been.

In light of the argument and the increasing agitation of the singer, such a shift would strike us as surprising and odd. This is close to what happens in Habakkuk 3.

As we come to the final chapter of Habakkuk's prophecy, we notice a significant shift in its structure. Chapters 1 and 2 are built around Habakkuk's two complaints against God and God's replies to Habakkuk. Then we get to chapter 3, and instead of another complaint, or anything even resembling the first two complaints, the prophet instead chooses to end with a song.

In the opening verse of chapter 3, we're told this is *"A prayer of Habakkuk the prophet, according to Shigionoth."* The meaning of "shigionoth" is a bit unclear, but most scholars believe it's some sort of ancient musical tune or accompaniment. The musical nature of these verses is confirmed at the end of the chapter (the very closing verse of the whole book) where we find another musical reference as Habakkuk directs this song: *"To the choirmaster: with stringed instruments."*

In the midst of the doubts and questions of this book, the prophet decides to end it not with a concise summary or solution to the problem of evil, not with a bare doctrinal answer, or even a restatement of the dilemma—but with a song. We'll come back to why Habakkuk switches his form, structure, and tone in this way. For now it's important to note that whatever the form and structure of chapter 3, the subject matter of this song is quite appropriate to the rest of the book. That's because the song found here is all about faith.

While the structure and form of the chapter are quite different from the rest of the book, this song of faith is a fitting way to end his writing. That's because throughout the three chapters of Habakkuk, the question of faith looms large. And Habakkuk is showing us that faith makes all the difference for people.

Faith Makes the Difference

One of the key verses in Habakkuk is found in 2:4, which declares, *"the righteous shall live by his faith."* This portion of 2:4 gets quoted three times in the New Testament[1] but the full text of this verse reads, *"Behold, his soul is puffed up within him, but the righteous shall live by his faith."*

This whole book of Scripture is about the question of faith, and this verse shows us that the opposite of faith is not doubt. As we have seen, Habakkuk teaches us that doubt can be an expression of faith. This is possible because the essence of faith is trust, and it's because Habakkuk trusts God that he goes to him with his doubts and complaints. He is troubled by what he sees happening around him and even by what God has to say about it all. However, because he has faith in God and because he trusts God's character and that God will listen, Habakkuk engages God with his doubt.

This is a very different way of life than the other people mentioned in this prophecy. The contrast in Habakkuk 2:4 shows us the true opposite of faith isn't doubt—it's pride. Habakkuk 2:4 is specifically addressing the nature of Babylonian pride. They are a people puffed up and swollen with self-importance.

Habakkuk 1 describes them as a vicious and cruel nation because their own might is their god. Trusting in their own strength and power, they see themselves as the arbiters of right and wrong. They trust only in themselves and in their own strength. They hold the ultimate "might makes right" approach to life, and since they have the might, they do as they please with no regard for others. Their understanding and their perspective is all that matters, and they are a strong nation so they just beat down anyone who disagrees or stands in their way. They are puffed up with self-regard, self-importance, and self-reliance. They are the epitome of pride.

Ultimately, the nation of Judah had this same problem. Habakkuk complains that Judah no longer trusts God. They don't listen to him or his word anymore. Their own opinion and judgment had become more important to them, so the law of God is paralyzed and justice is perverted. Their pride and self-importance has turned them into a culture of oppression and violence. In his original complaint against Judah, the prophet describes them in a way that sounds like they are becoming more like the faithless Babylonians in their outlook and way of life.

Faith and pride are the competing forces of the human psyche in this prophecy. With his doubts and complaints, Habakkuk could have gone either way. Out of pride, he could have assumed God had no answers or reasons for why he allowed the things he did. Out of self-importance, he could have assumed his perspective and understanding of the world was perfect, and he could have just complained *about* God instead of complaining *to* God. When God gave him an answer he didn't like, Habakkuk could have become puffed up with pride and presumed to act as a judge over God.

We all know Habakkuk could have responded in these ways because they are the ways we so often respond. Our default is to look at the events around us and in the world at large through the lens of our our incredibly limited wisdom and understanding. We declare that God can't be good or God can't be in control if he allows X to happen because there is obviously no point to it. And rather than allowing the grief and pain created by these things to turn us to God in humble dependence with our concerns, we often simply grumble and complain about him or about the raw deal he's given us. At least that's what I tend to do.

Habakkuk is different. He humbly trusts God is right and good even when he can't understand what God is doing. His faith makes all the difference for how he approaches life in this world. And he concludes his prophecy with a song expressing a deep and profound trust both in who God is and what he's able to do. As we look at this song, it teaches us much about what true faith looks like and what it does.

A Gritty Faith

In the Coen brothers 2010 remake of the classic Western *True Grit*, the young Mattie Ross tells Rooster Cogburn she sought him out because she was told he had real grit, which made him exactly the type of man to track down her father's killer in a lawless land.

The concept of grit is the basis of many a hero, or anti-hero, in most Westerns. However, grit is probably not a word we regularly associate with people of faith, but we should. Grit is precisely what we see in Habakkuk's faith, and it comes through in this closing song of his prophecy.

A person who has grit is someone who has a firmness of character. She isn't easily beaten down. A person of grit is determined and indomitable. He faces difficulties head on. Habakkuk is a person of grit, and he is gritty because of his faith. We've seen this already in Habakkuk 1-2.

Your faith has to have some grit if you have no real doubts about God's existence and power and yet you are still willing to get in God's face and say, "What's your problem?" And your faith has to have some grit when God actually responds to you, and you say, "Not good enough. What's your problem?" Which is basically a summary of Habakkuk's initial approach to God in this prophecy

We see even more true grit to Habakkuk's faith when we consider the words of his song carefully. Look at verse 16:

> *I hear, and my body trembles;*
> *my lips quiver at the sound;*
> *rottenness enters into my bones;*
> *my legs tremble beneath me.*

On the surface, this might not sound like grit to us. Trembling and quivering sound like weakness. But Habakkuk shows us that grit doesn't mean dishonesty.

Many people have a false bravado. They're big talkers until a real challenge or hardship comes their way. Many people do this with expressions of spirituality. A person can have a "faith bravado" that that talks a good game with all the right spiritual sounding words, but that can't ultimately stand up to real adversity.

That's not Habakkuk.

When Habakkuk says, "I hear," it is a reference back to all that God has told him in this book. He has heard what God has said, and he believes what he has heard. Since the whole first part of this song talks about the power, strength, and might of God—Habakkuk knows that if God says destruction is coming, then it's going to happen. God will do what he says he is going to do.

Habakkuk believes there is an impending judgment and doom that is going to fall on Judah. And where does Habakkuk live? In Judah. Where does everyone that Habakkuk knows live? In Judah.

In 3:16, we see Habakkuk is rightly broken up about all this. He is trembling and feels like he is physically falling apart because he knows that more pain and suffering are coming for his people.

If you've ever had to deliver terrible news to someone you love you know how hard it is. It tears you up so much emotionally and mentally that you feel it physically. This is what is happening to Habakkuk. Trembling and quivering is an honest and understandable response to the news he's received and is responsible to communicate to the people of Judah. The grit of his faith is seen in his willingness to accept all of this without sugarcoating it. There is no spiritualizing or minimizing of pain here, no clichéd mantra to dismiss the horrible news. Habakkuk accepts it all and faces it head on for what it is.

And yet there's more.

The gritty tenacity of Habakkuk's faith is also seen (3:16) when he says, *"Yet I will quietly wait for the day of trouble to come upon people who invade us."* This shows us he believes all of what God has said. Judgment will come on Judah, and they will be destroyed. But their destroyers will also be destroyed.

This wouldn't have been easy to believe. He's expressing a belief that the military superpower that is going to completely destroy and remove his nation will get its just reward. This would have been unthinkable for the average person in that day. It would be like telling someone tomorrow that within two years the United States, China, and Russia will no longer exist or exert influence on global politics.

Just imagine how hard it is for you to believe that God is right and just when people wrong you in minor ways. We think, "You don't know what you're doing. This can't possibly work out right or well. This person is just getting away with being a jerk." Yet, in the face of absolute crisis and destruction, Habakkuk trusts God will work it all out in his time.

And yet there's even more!

The full grit and tenacity of Habakkuk's faith is shown most clearly in verses 17–18:

> ¹⁷ *Though the fig tree should not blossom,*
> *nor fruit be on the vines,*
> *the produce of the olive fail*

and the fields yield no food,
the flock be cut off from the fold
and there be no herd in the stalls,
[18] yet I will rejoice in the LORD;
I will take joy in the God of my salvation.
[19] God, the Lord, is my strength;
he makes my feet like the deer's;
he makes me tread on my high places.

If you're familiar with Scripture you might have heard these words before. They are some of the most well-known words of Habakkuk and often one of the only parts of the book people recognize. People like these words and quote them because they sound inspiring.

While there certainly is something inspiring and uplifting in these words, I'm afraid they are often taken out of context and therefore understood in a way that is a bit saccharine and overly sentimental. In their original context, there is nothing sweet or easy in these verses. Habakkuk is describing complete and utter devastation.

Economic devastation.
Social devastation.
Famine, emptiness, want, despair.
Everything is ruined, everything is gone.
Everything is bleak.
All appears lost and hopeless.

In this setting Habakkuk sings, *"Yet I will rejoice in the Lord. I will take joy in the God of my salvation. God the Lord is my strength"* (3:18–19a).

This is so counter-intuitive to how we approach faith, particularly as Westerners. When our lives are going according to plan and working out decently, we find it easy to trust God. We know he's trustworthy when things are going well. When God seems to be answering my prayers in positive ways, then it's really easy to put my faith in him.

Habakkuk is saying the complete opposite. God is answering Habakkuk's prayers for deliverance with violence and destruction. He and his people will have nothing they want or need, nothing they've pled with God for.

No resources.
No food.
No security.
Absolutely nothing.
They are going to be wiped out.

Yet even in these circumstances, Habakkuk says he will not just believe in the Lord—he will rejoice in him. Habakkuk isn't just giving some sort of intellectual acknowledgement that God still exists. He says he will still delight in him. He will take joy in him. He will find comfort in this God, when there is no comfort anywhere else. That is a gritty faith.

There is an important lesson for us here in the grittiness of Habakkuk's faith precisely because it's so honest and real. Habakkuk is not painting false pictures of the way things are, or the way the world works. There is no escapism here. He's painting a picture of faithfulness and clinging to God in the midst of pain, suffering, and confusion at God's apparent inaction. This picture of faith is something Christianity needs, especially American Christianity. So much of American Christianity is soft and weak because it's just sweet sentimentalism. Our faith tends to lack grit.

This lack of grit might be seen most clearly in what is produced by the Christian sub-culture in the US. Just consider what types of books tend to be best-sellers in the Christian market. Most of them are light, fluffy, and ultimately a form of self-centered, infantilized spirituality.

Here's God's diet plan for your life.
Here's the secret to discovering God's plan to make you happy, healthy, and rich.
Here's how God is fitting into your understanding of the world.

It can also be seen in that markedly American heresy known as the Prosperity Gospel which teaches that you have the power to avoid all suffering through a warped understanding of faith. If you simply "name it and claim it" or "believe on the Lord for it" with enough faith then he must give you money, health, relationships, or whatever you want. In the Prosperity Gospel, God is a divine genie granting wishes. It's the spiritual version of the modern American pursuit of happiness.

This approach to faith cannot cope with the complex issues of suffering in this world. The Prosperity Gospel has no way to way to cope with the realities that God is all good and all powerful, and yet evil comes upon even truly faithful people. It's a corruption of true faith that leaves no room for legitimate doubts and uncertainties. Why do so many people who call themselves Christians buy the lie of the Prosperity Gospel? Maybe because it's an easy pill to swallow, it feels good going down. And we like easy answers that feel good. But there is no grit in that false faith because it is weakened through unrealistic expectations about what the life of faith is. As soon as difficulty comes in the front door, faith and trust in God can easily slip out the back door.

Take Christian art as another example (an abuse of the word "art" in most cases). Much of popular contemporary Christian art is often sappy and sentimental, kitschy, and tacky—precisely because it's too easy. The movies and the novels that get pushed out of evangelicalism are mostly full of simplistic clichés.

It's no wonder the American Church is hemorrhaging. Its people are largely being spoon-fed an anti-biblical faith that cannot stand up to reality. The garbage coming out of prosperity pulpits and the nonsense being peddled in the "Christian" marketplace is gutting the church from the inside out because all that is being offered are tasty placebos and colorfully decorated spiritual Band-Aids. This version of faith offers no true healing for the deep wounds and trauma that come from living in a sin ravaged world.

It's interesting and sadly ironic that I hear more Gospel truth coming out of many non-Christian cultural products than many so-called Christian ones. If you listen to the songs, watch the movies, or read the stories of many non-Christians you see a thirsting and hungering for some sort of real answer. They want something gritty that can actually engage them in the midst of the pain and the darkness they see.

Habakkuk is not sentimental. There are no easy cliché answers in this book nor anywhere else in the rest of Scripture. Scripture is real, and it doesn't pull any punches when it describes the reality of life in this world ransacked by evil. As individuals and as a church, we need to have a gritty, honest, real faith like Habakkuk's, or we won't be prepared to live in this world. We won't know what to do when everything falls apart. We also won't have anything to offer to anyone who is wrestling honestly with the darkness they see around them.

It's important to say though that I'm not suggesting anything like an unfeeling Stoicism when I'm talking about the grittiness of Habakkuk's faith. Habakkuk is not just hardening up or being tough and emotionless despite all difficulty. The short book of Habakkuk is emotionally charged. As he writes, it's clear he deeply feels all the pain, evil, and suffering he's writing about. He's not just putting on a strong face, but his faith in the face of all this has a strength we should admire. We may wonder how his faith can have such a realism and resolve to it in the face of all God has told him. This song shows us Habakkuk's resolve and grit come from the fact that his faith is also a remembering faith.

A Remembering Faith

If you read verses 1–15 of Habakkuk's song, it can seem a bit out of sync with the rest of the book. This is because the tone of those fifteen verses are triumphant and even celebratory. This is a song rejoicing and reveling in the strength, might, and power of God. This comes after two chapters of pain, frustration, anger, and the serious questioning of God's apparent inactivity.

However, when you realize what Habakkuk is doing in these verses, you see they're not out of place at all. In these triumphant verses, Habakkuk is not reflecting on what he has personally seen God do. Rather, he is remembering what God has done throughout history. We can see this is what Habakkuk is doing by the history he highlights.

In verse 3, we have a reference to Teman and Mount Paran. While these are unfamiliar names to most of us, they are actual places that would have been familiar to the original hearers of Habakkuk's message. Teman is in southern Palestine, and Mount Paran is in a mountain range a little further south in Teman on the eastern edge of the Sinai Peninsula. The reference to the tents of Cushan and the curtains of Midian are to the people who lived in that area ages ago. With these references, Habakkuk is looking back to God's formation of Israel in the Exodus as he led them out of Egypt in victory.

The Exodus was the supreme act of redemption and salvation in the Old Testament. It's where God most clearly displays his works of power. He brings the ten plagues upon Egypt (referenced in Habakkuk 3:5) and splits the seas so his people can walk across. Habakkuk is referencing this specific time period when God worked clearly, visibly, and undeniably. The places and the peoples of Cushan and Midian would have been the first ones to see Israel coming out of Egypt in triumph, which is why they trembled.

The imagery he uses in these verses highlights other historical acts of God and his constant care for his people. The pictures Habakkuk is painting with his words would have been familiar to his audience because they are the typical images used throughout Scripture to describe God's victory and his work in the world.

Habakkuk 3 sounds similar to the songs of Moses and Miriam in Exodus 15. It's also connected to Deuteronomy 33, where Moses reflects on God's care for his people during their wilderness wandering.

The language here in Habakkuk is also strikingly close to some of the language from Deborah's song of praise to God for his victory over their Canaanite oppressors in Judges 5. In that passage, we read about God marching through the earth with the mountains quaking and trembling before him.

Most interestingly, Habakkuk 3 is almost identical to Psalm 77, which teaches that there will be a day of trouble, a time of affliction and suffering. Psalm 77 instructs us to remember all God has done. The lesson here is that in order to move forward in faith, we must look behind us in history to see how God has worked salvation in the past. This is what Habakkuk is doing in chapter 3.

In this song, Habakkuk is not trying to identify just one or two historical events. Rather, he is putting together a verbal collage, a mosaic of various historical events. He does this to paint a clear picture of a God who fights for his people. In this way, he reminds his readers that when God fights for his people, he wins. This remembering grounds Habakkuk's faith and gives it that gritty strength.

All of this shows us Habakkuk's faith isn't blind optimism. It's not wishful thinking in the midst of evil and suffering. It's rooted in an understanding of history. He's trusting in the God who is, and the God he knows exists because he has worked and acted in history. This is the God who has spoken promises to his people and proven he is both willing and able to fulfill those promises.

One commentator sums it up this way: "Remembering the past gives an anchor for the present as the faithful wait for the future."[2] Remembering the past and God's work *then* provides a steadying anchor for us to hold on to in the midst of whatever storms of life we're facing *now* as we wait for his full work to be done in the *future*. Through this song Habakkuk remembers, and he is calling God's people to remember, that though God doesn't work according to our timing, and though he doesn't work according to our preferences, he does work. God does act.

Habakkuk knows, trusts, and remembers that God is this kind of God, a God who still goes out for the salvation of his people. This gives him hope even in the face of impending judgment. It enables him to prayerfully sing, *"In wrath remember mercy"* (3:2). Habakkuk is remembering God's promise to remember his promises. This remembering of Habakkuk is what makes his faith gritty because he remembers that God does indeed act. God does destroy the wicked, AND God does remember his promise of salvation. Because of this, Habakkuk is able to remain firm. He knows his faith isn't just naïve, wishful thinking.

Habakkuk doesn't see God working in his day, but he

remembers that God work for his people. He sees no evidence that God is really present, but he remembers what God has done in the past. So he clings to him. With all his doubts and with all his concerns and complaints. Habakkuk remembers who this God is and trusts him. He makes God's history of acting his hope and rests fully on him. This assurance of how God has acted in the past becomes more central to him than even his present circumstances.

Therefore, even though everything around him is falling apart, even though everything around him is coming undone and coming to nothing, he is able to cry out: *"yet I will rejoice in the LORD. I will take joy in the God of my salvation. God, the LORD, is my strength."*

We can do the same. We can practice a remembering faith. We can cry out, "Yet I will rejoice in the Lord"—not in my circumstances. We can practice saying, "I will take joy in the God of my salvation" because he is permanent, and he is unchanging even when the world around us trembles and quakes. We can admit our feelings are precarious and our circumstances are as stable as a sand castle on a stormy sea. Nothing easy is promised to us. Yet we need not fear because God is immovable. He is the stability we need. We can declare these things, not as empty words but as confident hope. When we do what Habakkuk is calling us to do—practice a remembering faith.

This is what Christians are called to do week by week in corporate worship. Through the liturgy of worship, we rehearse the Gospel and remember God's actions throughout history. We worship weekly because we need a regular reminder of who this God is and what he has done.

I often begin our weekly worship by saying something to the effect of, "We gather together today to remember who God is and therefore who we are." We give a profession of faith every week to clearly recall who this God is and what he has done. We have a call to repentance and an assurance of grace to remember that, though our sins are present and real, so is God's grace. We have this liturgy because it forms us and helps us to remember all we so easily forget. We are afflicted with a spiritual amnesia, and every time we walk out the door from worship, we tend to forgot it all. We have to come back week after week to be restored and renewed by remembering.

This is also why the majority of Christians around the world make at least some use of the liturgical calendar, recognizing the great works of God's salvation regularly throughout the year. It's not that these days are somehow more holy or sacred than other days. We emphasize these special days by setting aside dedicated time to celebrate the memory of these events in order to weave them more deeply into the fabric of our experience. We make the remembering of this history a regular part of our approach to life in this world.

We celebrate Advent and Christmas to remember that God has visited this world in the flesh, and remembering gives us faith and hope as we wait for him to come back. We celebrate Good Friday and Easter Sunday to remember that our sin and the evil of the world have already been decisively dealt with in history. We celebrate these days and seasons to remind ourselves these things actually happened. The death of death in the resurrection of Jesus has a date attached to it. We celebrate these days to remember Christianity is not a theoretical religion built around ideals. It's a living faith that trusts in the God who acts in history.

It's essential that we do these things and remember this is the God we serve because, like Habakkuk, we don't see God working in our day. At least not with acts of might and power and not with a clear and visible hand.

God doesn't detail the ways he's working on the nightly news. He has never sent you a text saying, "Here's exactly what I'm doing in these circumstances of your life." Because of this, God can seem very far away, especially when we are in emotional pain. Meanwhile, evil seems to have the upper hand. And injustice, corruption, violence, destruction, sickness, suffering, and death surround us clearly and visibly. Like Habakkuk we cry out "How long, O Lord? Why don't you do something? Don't you care?" And as an answer to those questions, he calls us to remember what he has done so we will know he cares.

In rehearsing and remembering the Gospel, we recall that God secured the salvation of his people. He came to crush the head of the wicked one and destroy his reign. He used all his power for the rescue of his people. With grit, Jesus trusted his Father and went to the cross. He came as the servant king, who was the one laid bare from thigh to neck (3:13), taking the place of the wicked, and receiving our judgment. Jesus receives wrath for us so that God will remember mercy (3:2). And in his resurrection, Jesus promised us his work wasn't done. Just as he acted decisively in history, he will return in the future to decisively remove all suffering with his resurrection power (Revelation 21:4).

As we wait for the completion of what Jesus will do we must look back to what he has done. When we remember these things, we are able to cling to him like Habakkuk— with all our doubts, with all our concerns and complaints. We remember who God is and trust him, and this remembering can help imbue our faith with grit. Even though everything around us may be falling apart, everything may be coming undone, we know God isn't aloof and uncaring about the evil of this world. He knows it intimately because he entered into it and suffered it for us. When we remember this, it won't answer all of our questions but it will allow us to declare with Hababkkuk: *"yet I will rejoice in the LORD. I will take joy in the God of my salvation. God, the Lord, is my strength."*

A Sung Faith

There's one last important point we need to consider. Habakkuk's faith is not just a gritty faith, and it's not just a remembering faith. It's a sung faith. I don't know how many times I read Habakkuk before I preached through it for the first time, but until that point, I never really gave much thought to the way this short book of the Bible ends. It finishes with a song, which is remarkable.

Habakkuk has been wrestling with these huge issues of life and faith: the problem of evil, the problem of suffering, and the problem of God's apparent silence in the face of these things. Isn't it interesting then that, as he concludes, he doesn't give us what we might think we want?

He doesn't give us a dry theological dissertation seeking to explain away these problems. Habakkuk doesn't give us a philosophical treatise or rationale trying to make sense of it all. He gives us a song. In the face of the hardest questions, he gives us something to sing. I think that's a profoundly pastoral way to conclude.

I mentioned earlier that there really is no satisfying rational answer to the problem of evil. That's because the problem of evil ultimately is not rational. Evil doesn't make sense. But there's something more to the absence of an answer here. Often times when I'm talking with people about the problem of evil, I can give all sorts of answers (or at least partial answers), but they're so intellectual and heady that they just don't seem to help. What I often say to people is that these are "head answers" to "heart questions." What I mean by that is that if you are in a season where you are really wrestling with the problem of evil, if it's a personal struggle for you—then it's not something you're thinking about, it's something you're feeling. It's something that's churning you up inside. If that's the case then a head answer won't ultimately help you in the moment of your pain.

As a pastor, I get asked many difficult questions. Sometimes I have what I think are pretty good answers. I've thought through them. I've studied hard to give biblically sound and theologically accurate answers. But even the best answers can be deeply unsatisfying. That's because head-answers aren't always the best replies to heart-questions. And pastors fail to care well for people if all we do is give head-answers to questions coming from the heart.

This shouldn't surprise us because we are not merely rational beings. We are people of deep emotions and even deeper longings which go beyond the merely intellectual and often beyond even our conscious awareness. This is why the end of Habakkuk is surprisingly beautiful. God's response to the problem of evil is not an algorithm or equation. It's not a sermon or theological solutions to go and think harder about.

Instead, he gives us a song. He says, "Sing this and remember." Perhaps this is because singing can form us and answer our heart-questions in ways our heads can't fully comprehend.

My friend Kevin Twit is a campus minister at Belmont University. He has spearheaded the development of a group of musicians known as Indelible Grace[3] which has been influential in bringing new life to old Christian hymns.

When it comes to the importance of singing, Kevin points out that singing intensifies whatever we are doing, whether praise or lament. This intensification comes about because of the nature of singing. Kevin describes singing as an embodied activity in which sound resonates through our bodies. Singing in worship is a communal activity because as we sing together, we hear one another in the midst of the gathering of God's people. In these ways, singing takes the words which are sung beyond mere intellectual recitation, and it drives them more deeply into the core of our being.

This is how God has designed the human experience of

singing and why he's always included it as a central element in our worship of him. Highlighting the importance of singing in the Christian faith author Reggie Kidd has written, "A theology that cannot be sung is not worth having…. Authentic Christian faith is not merely believed. Nor is it merely acted upon. It is sung—with utter joy sometimes, in uncontrollable tears sometimes, but it is sung."[4] There's an ancient saying which has been widely attributed to Saint Augustine that summarizes this intensifying and central role of singing to faith: "He who sings, prays twice."

I mentioned above the importance of regular worship for remembering who God is and what he has done in history. This is also why singing is such an important part of our worship. Through song, we approach God with our whole person—head, heart, and body. As we sing, this remembering of his person and his actions is not just an intellectual exercise; it's a whole person experience. We sing his praise, his adoration, our lament, and our thanks. As we sing these things, the reality of his goodness and grace is woven more deeply into our being. Through the practice of singing, God's goodness and faithfulness become more fully a part of our conscious thinking, but they also begin to reshape our deepest hopes and longings by speaking comfort into the hidden parts of our heart.

This is why one of my biggest concerns as a pastor is how common it is for believers to skip out on corporate worship and why I talk with people frequently about the importance of being regular and consistent in public worship.[5] In my experience regularly worshipping with God's people is one of the most neglected aspects of

Christian discipleship in the West. And yet it's the most central and primary place of Christian discipleship. A large part of its centrality in discipleship is because it's the time and place where you learn to sing your faith and therefore come to remember and believe that faith more fully.

Weekly worship is not just about attendance. It's not a matter of checking something off a list of religious duties. You need to worship weekly because you need Jesus. You need to see that Jesus is ultimately God's answer to the evil and suffering of the world. And Jesus will be more real to you when you gather together with others and sing to him than when you sit alone and think about him.

I'm not saying privately thinking through the faith is unimportant. That couldn't be further from the truth. It's deeply important that people meditate on the truths and promises of Scripture. You need to grasp the historicity of the Gospel in order to grow in the faith. That takes some mental wrestling through tough bits of history and theology.

However, that's not enough, especially in moments of doubt and distress. When you are silent and alone, your problems and those of the world will loom large. When you get stuck in your own head, you won't be able to see the real problems of life in this world with the proper perspective.

Corporate worship takes us out of ourselves, particularly when we're singing. Participating in the gathered worship of the Church isn't some magic bullet to remove all doubt, but cutting yourself off from it will make all your problems seem bigger than God. It's in the regular worship of God, publicly with others, that we learn how to be faithful with our doubts.

When you gather together with others, you are reminded you are not alone. There are other people who have been shaped by this same story. When you worship and sing praise to the Lord of Life who triumphed o'er the grave, the one who rose victorious in the strife for those he came to save—you'll find greater joy and comfort in the one who died to bring eternal life and lives that death may die.[6] When you sing about how his perfect love will never change, and his mercies never cease, you will experience more fully the hope of his peace, and you will be empowered to actually rejoice.[7]

Singing God's praise won't remove your questions. Singing won't remove your doubts or your complaints against him. But it will put them in their place. As you worshipfully remember what your risen King has done, you will develop a grit that enables you to carry on in the face of adversity. But you will also find encouragement in the midst of despair, comfort in the midst of pain, and faith in the midst of doubt.

This is why the Holy Spirit inspired Habakkuk to end his book with this song of gritty, remembering faith. Not merely to fill our heads but to develop our hearts. With that in mind, maybe the best way to conclude is to share one of my favorite songs about God's work on our behalf in the midst of a world of suffering and pain, *Our Help In Ages Past*, by Isaac Watts:

> O God, our help in ages past,
> Our hope for years to come,

Our shelter from the stormy blast,
And our eternal home.

Under the shadow of Thy throne
Thy saints have dwelt secure;
Sufficient is Thine arm alone,
And our defense is sure.

Before the hills in order stood,
Or earth received her frame,
From everlasting Thou art God,
To endless years the same.

O God, our help in ages past,
Our hope for years to come,
Be Thou our guard while troubles last,
And our eternal home.

———

Questions for Reflection

1. What do you think about the statement that the opposite of faith isn't doubt but pride?
2. Discuss the concept of "gritty" faith? How does Habakkuk demonstrate grit in his faith? In your life, do you know anyone who is an example of gritty faith? How has their example of gritty faith inspired or strengthened you?
3. In your own words how would you describe the

difference between a "blind optimism" and a "remembering faith"? How does Habakkuk's remembering faith give him a gritty faith? What might this look like for a Christian? How can you seek to better practice a remembering faith?

4. What do you think about the idea that singing forms us and answers our concerns in ways that our heads can't comprehend? Have you experienced this at all in your own walk with Christ?

5. What are your thoughts on the importance of having a "sung" faith? Do you regularly sing your faith in worship and if so, how does that experience impact your questions and doubts?

---

1. See Romans 1:17; Galatians 3:11; Hebrews 10:37.
2. Bruckner, *Jonah, Nahum, Habakkuk, Zephaniah*, 261.
3. For more information on Indelible Grace go to igracemusic.com.
4. Reggie M. Kidd, *With One Voice: Discovering Christ's Song in Our Worship* (Grand Rapids: Baker Books, 2005), 13.
5. Declaring the importance of regular and consistent weekly public worship is not meant to diminish the painful struggle this presents for many people. There are many who've dropped out of public worship because they've been wounded by the church. It's an unfortunate fact that not every congregation is a safe place to express and explore faithful doubt. However, corporate worship still remains the primary place in God's economy to be built up in the faith so I'd urge you to find a safe and healthy church to join with for regular public worship so you can sing your faith with other believers.
6. See *Crown Him With Many Crowns*.
7. See *Come People of the Risen King*.

CLOSING THOUGHTS

I believe. Help my unbelief.
—Mark 9:24

I first preached through the book of Habakkuk in the winter of 2018. Later that year, a friend encouraged me to consider adapting those messages into this little book. Due to a variety of circumstances, my own procrastination chief among them, the work of adapting and editing has stretched from 2018 into 2020. Suffice it to say, when I originally preached on Habakkuk in 2018 and then began developing those messages into this little primer on faithful doubt, I had no what idea lay ahead in 2020. A global pandemic, more police brutality, nationwide protests and civil unrest, increasing political polarization, the fear of an impending economic collapse, hurricanes, wildfires, and even murder hornets—it has been quite a year of wrestling with God in faithful doubt for myself and so many others.

Yet, I have found this timing helpful for me. Enduring

all these things, and pastoring a church through them while writing about Habakkuk, has forced me to wrestle once again with whether I really believe all the things I've written here are true. I have found again that I do.

Like Habakkuk, I have my own faithful doubts. I have questions and complaints for God. And I'm one in a long line of people for whom the extreme circumstances of 2020 has exacerbated my faithful doubt. This has always been the way of things. Habakkuk lived in extreme circumstances, and God told him more were on the way. These provoked his concerns and doubts. These created a crisis and gave him the critical choice—either move toward God or move away from him. By God's grace, I continue to move toward him, or at least, I continue to desire to move toward him.

If you've read through this little book, you are likely wrestling with your own questions and doubts, if not outright complaints about God. I hope this work has helped you decide to continue moving toward him. I encourage you to follow Habakkuk's example and complain to God in faith rather than about him in cynical pride. Trust me when I say that I don't say that lightly. I know all too well the allure of cynical pride.

If you're desiring to move toward God in faithful doubt, the best thing you can do is simply to talk to him about all your questions, doubts, and complaints. The second best thing you can do is find a Christian friend or leader who is safe and understanding and try to verbalize and process your struggles with them. Perhaps you can work through some of the reflection questions included in the book. Find some other Christians to help you discuss and think through the things troubling you. The Christian life is not meant to be lived as a solo adventure. And if you don't already have one, I'd urge you to find a church where you can sing your faith with other believers. Or maybe even begin to develop a new faith through singing and worship. Faith is meant to be lived out in community, and our doubts are meant to be tackled in community, not borne alone in private pain.

Finally, I want to thank you for taking the time to read and consider what I've written, especially if you are currently in a place of struggle and uncertainty. I know that even taking the step of reading something about this subject can be difficult because you're opening yourself up to the possibility of disappointment. Thank you for your vulnerability. I hope you weren't disappointed. I pray these words, inadequate as they are, might be used to bring some comfort and hope to you in the midst of your heart-questions.

BIBLIOGRAPHY

James Bruckner, The NIV Application Commentary: Jonah, Nahum, Habakkuk, Zephaniah, (Grand Rapids: Zondervan), 2004.

Os Guiness, Doubt: Faith In Two Minds, (Herts, England: Lion Publishing), 1983.

Riad A. Kassis, Frustrated with God: A Syrian Theologian's Reflections on Habakkuk, (Riad A. Kassis), 2016.

Timothy Keller, The Reason for God: Belief in an Age of Skepticism, (New York: Dutton), 2008.

Reggie M. Kidd, With One Voice: Discovering Christ's Song in Our Worship, (Grand Rapids: Baker Books), 2005.

C. S. Lewis, The Lion, the Witch, and the Wardrobe, (New York: HarperCollins), 1978.

N. T. Wright, Evil and the Justice of God, (Downers Grove: InterVarsity), 2006.

ABOUT THE AUTHOR

Travis is the pastor of Grace & Peace Presbyterian Church in Pittsburgh, Pennsylvania. Prior to that, he was a missionary in Auckland, New Zealand, where he served as a church planter and taught practical theology at Grace Theological College.

Besides spending time with his family, Travis enjoys drinking excessive amounts of coffee, less excessive amounts of gin and tonic, developing his subpar skills in woodworking, watching good movies, listening to *Murder By Death*, slaying orcs and bugbears, and drinking more coffee. He is a founding member of The Order of Balaam's Ass.

ALSO BY WHITE BLACKBIRD BOOKS

All Are Welcome: Toward a Multi-Everything Church

The Almost Dancer

Birth of Joy: Philippians

Choosing a Church: A Biblical and Practical Guide

Christ in the Time of Corona: Stories of Faith, Hope, and Love

Co-Laborers, Co-Heirs: A Family Conversation

Doing God's Work

EmbRACE: A Biblical Study on Justice and Race

Ever Light and Dark: Telling Secrets, Telling the Truth

Everything Is Meaningless? Ecclesiastes

Heal Us Emmanuel: A Call for Racial Reconciliation, Representation, and Unity in the Church

Hear Us, Emmanuel: Another Call for Racial Reconciliation, Representation, and Unity in the Church

The Organized Pastor: Systems to Care for People Well

Questions of the Heart: Leaning In, Listening For, and Loving Well Toward True Identity in Christ

Rooted: The Apostles' Creed

A Sometimes Stumbling Life

To You I Lift Up My Soul: Confessions and Prayers

Urban Hinterlands: Planting the Gospel in Uncool Places

Follow whiteblackbirdbooks.pub for titles and releases.

ABOUT WHITE BLACKBIRD BOOKS

White blackbirds are extremely rare, but they are real. They are blackbirds that have turned white over the years as their feathers have come in and out over and over again. They are a redemptive picture of something you would never expect to see but that has slowly come into existence over time.

There is plenty of hurt and brokenness in the world. There is the hopelessness that comes in the midst of lost jobs, lost health, lost homes, lost marriages, lost children, lost parents, lost dreams, loss.

But there also are many white blackbirds. There are healed marriages, children who come home, friends who are reconciled. There are hurts healed, children fostered and adopted, communities restored. Some would call these events entirely natural, but really they are unexpected miracles.

The books in this series are not commentaries, nor are they meant to be the final word. Rather, they are a collage of biblical truth applied to current times and places. The authors share their poverty and trust the Lord to use their words to strengthen and encourage his people. Consider these books as entries into the discussion.

May this series help you in your quest to know Christ as he is found in the Gospel through the Scriptures. May you look for and even expect the rare white blackbirds of God's redemption through Christ in your midst. May you be thankful when you look down and see your feathers have turned. May you also rejoice when you see that others have been unexpectedly transformed by Jesus.